System Design
100 Interview Questions

X.Y. Wang

Contents

4 **Advanced** 77

Chapter 1

Introduction

System design is an essential aspect of the software development process, with a significant impact on the performance, scalability, and reliability of any software application. As the world moves towards an increasingly interconnected and data-driven environment, the need for well-designed and robust systems has become critical. In recent years, the importance of system design in the software engineering domain has only grown, leading to a greater emphasis on system design interviews for software engineering positions.

"System Design: 100 Interview Questions" is a comprehensive guide for software engineers, architects, and professionals seeking to hone their system design skills and prepare for technical interviews. This book covers a wide range of topics, from the basics of distributed systems to advanced concepts such as globally distributed, multi-region systems, and machine learning models in a distributed environment.

Structured in five sections—Basic, Intermediate, Advanced, Expert, and Guru—this book provides 100 carefully curated questions and answers designed to challenge and refine the reader's understanding of various system design concepts. Each question is followed by a detailed explanation that delves into the underlying principles, best practices, and potential trade-offs associated with the topic. As you progress through the book, the questions become increasingly complex, allowing you to apply your newfound knowledge to more intricate system design challenges.

The Basic section provides an overview of fundamental concepts, such as system design, functional and non-functional requirements, high-level and low-level design, common components of distributed systems, and the importance of scalability, among others. This section lays a strong foundation for understanding the core principles of system design.

The Intermediate section delves into more complex topics, such as sharding, RESTful APIs, design patterns, data consistency, and performance optimization. This section helps to solidify the reader's understanding of essential system design techniques and strategies.

The Advanced section covers an array of topics, including backpressure, schema changes and migrations, rate limiting, versioning, and various consistency models. This section prepares the reader to tackle more sophisticated system design problems.

The Expert section explores advanced concepts, such as globally distributed systems, multi-tenancy, data deduplication, long-running transactions, and end-to-end encryption. This section offers valuable insights for designing complex, large-scale systems.

Lastly, the Guru section delves into cutting-edge topics like linearizability, advanced data processing, geo-replication, advanced security, and distributed machine learning. This section challenges the reader to consider and master the most advanced aspects of system design.

"System Design: 100 Interview Questions" is an invaluable resource for anyone seeking to deepen their understanding of system design, enhance their problem-solving skills, and prepare for technical interviews. Whether you are a beginner or an experienced professional, this book offers a wealth of knowledge to help you excel in your system design journey. So, let's embark on this intellectual adventure and unlock the secrets of designing efficient, scalable, and reliable systems.

Chapter 2

Basic

2.1 What is a system design? Can you provide a brief overview?

System design refers to the process of defining, developing, and implementing a system that meets certain requirements. A system can be any collection of components that work together to achieve a specific goal, such as a software application, a website, or a mechanical device. The goal of system design is to create a solution that is efficient, effective, and meets the needs of the users.

The system design process typically involves several steps, including:

Requirements gathering: This is the process of identifying the needs and goals of the system. This may involve talking to stakeholders, analyzing data, and conducting user research.

Design: This involves creating a plan for how the system will be built. This may involve creating diagrams, flowcharts, or other visual aids to help communicate the design.

Development: This is the process of actually building the system, which may involve writing code, creating graphics, or building physical components.

Testing: Once the system is built, it needs to be tested to ensure that it meets the requirements and works as expected.

Deployment: This is the process of releasing the system to users.

Maintenance: Once the system is in use, it may require ongoing maintenance to ensure that it continues to work as expected.

Here is an example to illustrate the system design process:

Suppose a company wants to build a mobile app that allows users to order food from local restaurants. The system design process might involve the following steps:

Requirements gathering: The company would talk to users and stakeholders to identify the features and functionality that the app should include. This might include the ability to browse menus, place orders, and track deliveries.

Design: The company would create a plan for how the app will be built, including wireframes and user flows to help communicate the design.

Development: The company would build the app, which might involve writing code, creating graphics, and integrating with third-party APIs for payment processing and restaurant data.

Testing: The company would test the app to ensure that it meets the requirements and works as expected. This might involve conducting user testing and bug testing.

Deployment: Once the app is tested and ready, the company would release it to users through app stores.

Maintenance: The company would continue to maintain the app, fixing bugs and adding new features as needed.

Overall, system design is a critical process that helps ensure that systems are built efficiently and effectively to meet the needs of users.

2.2   Can you differentiate between functional and non-functional requirements?

Functional requirements and non-functional requirements are two different types of requirements that are often defined during the system design process.

Functional requirements are requirements that describe the specific features and functions that a system must have in order to meet its goals. These requirements define what the system should do, and are typically related to the specific tasks that the system is designed to perform. Examples of functional requirements might include:

The ability to add items to a shopping cart The ability to search for products by keyword The ability to process payments through a third-party payment gateway

Non-functional requirements, on the other hand, are requirements that describe how the system should perform. These requirements are not related to the specific features and functions of the system, but rather to its overall performance, security, and usability. Examples of non-functional requirements might include:

Response time: The system must respond to user requests within 2 seconds. Scalability: The system must be able to handle a large number of users simultaneously without slowing down. Security: The system must protect user data from unauthorized access or disclosure.

Here is an example to illustrate the difference between functional and non-functional requirements:

Suppose a company is designing an e-commerce website. The functional requirements might include:

- The ability to browse products by category

- The ability to add products to a shopping cart

- The ability to process payments through a third-party payment gateway

The non-functional requirements for the same e-commerce website might include:

- Response time: The website must load pages within 3 seconds.

- Scalability: The website must be able to handle 10,000 simultaneous users.

- Usability: The website must be easy to navigate and use for users of all skill levels.

In summary, functional requirements describe what a system should do, while non-functional requirements describe how a system should perform. Both types of requirements are important for designing a system that meets the needs of its users and performs effectively.

2.3   What is the difference between high-level design and low-level design?

High-level design and low-level design are two different levels of system design that are often defined during the system design process.

High-level design, also known as architectural design, is the process of defining the overall structure and organization of a system. This includes identifying the major components of the system, their relationships to each other, and the interfaces between them. High-level design focuses on the system's functionality, performance, and scalability. Examples of high-level design might include:

- Identifying the major modules or components of a software system and their relationships to each other

- Designing the overall architecture of a database system, including how data is organized and accessed

- Designing the network architecture for a distributed system, including how nodes communicate with each other

Low-level design, on the other hand, is the process of specifying the details of how individual components of a system will be implemented.

This includes defining algorithms, data structures, and specific implementation details. Low-level design focuses on the system's reliability, maintainability, and testability. Examples of low-level design might include:

- Defining the data structures and algorithms used by a particular module of a software system

- Specifying the syntax and semantics of programming language constructs

- Defining the protocols used for communication between nodes in a distributed system

Here is an example to illustrate the difference between high-level and low-level design:

Suppose a company is designing a web application for managing a database of customer information. The high-level design might include:

- Identifying the major components of the system, such as the user interface, database, and application server

- Defining the interfaces between these components, such as the API used to access the database

- Designing the overall architecture of the system, such as a three-tier architecture with a web front-end, application server, and database backend

The low-level design for the same web application might include:

- Defining the data structures used by the database, such as tables, columns, and indexes

- Specifying the algorithms used for querying the database, such as SQL statements

- Defining the user interface components, such as HTML forms and JavaScript functions, used for data entry and display

In summary, high-level design defines the overall structure and organization of a system, while low-level design specifies the details of how individual components will be implemented. Both levels of design are important for creating a system that meets the needs of its users and performs effectively.

2.4 What are some common components of a distributed system?

A distributed system is a system in which components located on different computers communicate and coordinate their actions by passing messages. Distributed systems are used in a variety of applications, including cloud computing, peer-to-peer file sharing, and distributed databases. Here are some common components of a distributed system:

Nodes: Nodes are the individual computers or servers that make up a distributed system. Each node has its own processing power and memory, and can communicate with other nodes over a network.

Network: The network is the infrastructure that connects the nodes in a distributed system. This may be a local area network (LAN), wide area network (WAN), or the internet.

Middleware: Middleware is software that sits between the application and the operating system, providing services such as message passing, remote procedure calls, and distributed file systems. Examples of middleware include Apache Kafka, RabbitMQ, and Apache Cassandra.

Protocols: Protocols are a set of rules for communication between nodes in a distributed system. They define the format of messages, the order of messages, and the actions to be taken in response to certain events. Examples of protocols used in distributed systems include HTTP, TCP, and UDP.

Load balancers: Load balancers are used to distribute incoming traffic across multiple nodes in a distributed system, ensuring that no single node becomes overloaded. Load balancers can be implemented in hardware or software, and can be configured to use different algorithms for distributing traffic.

Distributed databases: Distributed databases are databases that are spread across multiple nodes in a distributed system. This allows for faster data access and more resilient data storage, since data can be replicated across multiple nodes.

Security mechanisms: Security mechanisms are used to protect data and prevent unauthorized access in a distributed system. This may include encryption, access control, and authentication mechanisms.

Here is an example to illustrate the components of a distributed system:

Suppose a company is building a distributed system for processing credit card transactions. The components of the system might include:

Nodes: The system might consist of multiple nodes, each of which is responsible for processing a subset of the transactions.

Network: The nodes would communicate with each other over a network, which might be the internet or a private network.

Middleware: The system might use middleware such as Apache Kafka to handle message passing between nodes.

Protocols: The system might use protocols such as TCP or HTTP to ensure reliable communication between nodes.

Load balancers: The system might use load balancers to distribute incoming transactions across multiple nodes.

Distributed databases: The system might use a distributed database such as Apache Cassandra to store transaction data across multiple nodes.

Security mechanisms: The system would use encryption and authentication mechanisms to protect transaction data and prevent unauthorized access.

In summary, a distributed system consists of multiple components working together to achieve a common goal. These components include nodes, networks, middleware, protocols, load balancers, distributed databases, and security mechanisms. By understanding these components, designers can build distributed systems that are efficient, resilient, and secure.

2.5 What is the importance of scalability in system design? How can you achieve it?

Scalability is the ability of a system to handle an increasing amount of work or traffic. In system design, scalability is important because it allows a system to grow and adapt to changing needs over time. Without scalability, a system may become overwhelmed and unable to perform its intended functions as the number of users or transactions increases.

There are several reasons why scalability is important in system design:

Future growth: A system that is designed to be scalable can accommodate future growth and changing user needs without requiring a complete redesign.

Cost-effectiveness: A scalable system can be more cost-effective than a non-scalable system, since it may be possible to add resources as needed rather than investing in a large, upfront infrastructure.

Availability: A scalable system can be designed to provide high availability, ensuring that users can access the system even during peak usage periods.

Achieving scalability in system design requires careful planning and consideration of several factors:

Horizontal scaling: Horizontal scaling involves adding more nodes or servers to a system to handle increasing load. This approach is often used for web applications, where additional servers can be added to a load balancer to handle increased traffic.

Vertical scaling: Vertical scaling involves adding more resources to a single server or node, such as adding more memory or processing power. This approach may be more appropriate for applications that require more processing power or memory rather than simply handling more users.

Design for modularity: Designing a system with modular components can make it easier to add or remove components as needed to scale the system.

Design for fault tolerance: A system that is designed to be fault tolerant can recover from failures more quickly and provide more consistent performance, which is important for ensuring scalability.

Use distributed systems: A distributed system can help achieve scalability by distributing the workload across multiple nodes or servers.

Here is an example to illustrate the importance of scalability in system design and how it can be achieved:

Suppose a company is designing a social media platform that it expects to grow rapidly in the coming years. To achieve scalability, the system might be designed with the following considerations:

Horizontal scaling: The system might be designed to scale horizontally by adding more servers to handle increasing traffic. This might involve using load balancers to distribute traffic across multiple servers.

Design for modularity: The system might be designed with modular components, such as separate servers for handling user authentication and user data storage. This would make it easier to add or remove components as needed to scale the system.

Use distributed systems: The system might be designed as a distributed system, with different servers handling different tasks, such as processing user posts, handling user messages, or managing user authentication.

Design for fault tolerance: The system might be designed with fault tolerance in mind, such as using redundant servers to ensure that the system can recover from failures quickly.

By considering these factors, the social media platform can be designed to be scalable and accommodate growth in users and traffic over time.

In summary, scalability is an important consideration in system design, as it allows a system to handle increasing amounts of work or traffic. Achieving scalability requires careful planning and consideration of factors such as horizontal and vertical scaling, modularity, fault tolerance, and distributed systems.

2.6 Can you explain the concept of horizontal and vertical scaling?

Horizontal and vertical scaling are two different approaches to scaling a system to handle increasing workloads or traffic.

Vertical scaling involves adding more resources to a single node or server to handle increased load. This may involve adding more memory, processing power, or storage capacity to a single server. Vertical scaling is often used when a system requires more processing power or memory rather than simply handling more users. Here are some examples of vertical scaling:

Adding more RAM to a server to handle more simultaneous connections Upgrading the CPU of a server to improve processing speed Adding more storage to a server to accommodate more data

Vertical scaling can be limited by the capacity of the hardware, and may eventually become more expensive than horizontal scaling.

Horizontal scaling involves adding more nodes or servers to a system to handle increased load. This approach is often used for web applications or other systems that require handling a large number of simultaneous users. Here are some examples of horizontal scaling:

Adding more servers to a load balancer to handle increased traffic Sharding a database by distributing data across multiple servers Using a distributed file system to store and access large amounts of data

Horizontal scaling can be more cost-effective than vertical scaling, as it allows a system to grow incrementally by adding additional servers as needed.

Here is an example to illustrate the difference between horizontal and vertical scaling:

Suppose a company is designing an e-commerce website that expects to handle increasing amounts of traffic as it grows. To achieve scalability, the company might consider the following approaches:

Vertical scaling: The company might upgrade the CPU and memory of its existing server to handle increased traffic. This would be an example of vertical scaling.

Horizontal scaling: The company might add additional servers to a load balancer to handle increased traffic. This would be an example of horizontal scaling.

By considering both approaches, the company can achieve scalability in different ways depending on its specific needs and constraints.

In summary, vertical scaling involves adding more resources to a single node or server, while horizontal scaling involves adding more nodes or servers to a system. Both approaches are used to achieve scalability and handle increasing workloads or traffic. The choice of approach will depend on factors such as the system's architecture, the type of workload, and cost constraints.

2.7 What is caching and why is it important in system design?

Caching is the process of storing frequently accessed data in a high-speed storage system in order to reduce the time and resources required to access that data from the original source. Caching is important in system design because it can significantly improve the performance and scalability of a system by reducing the load on the original data source.

Caching works by storing frequently accessed data in a cache, which is typically a high-speed storage system such as RAM or solid-state drives (SSDs). When data is requested, the system first checks the cache to see if the data is available. If the data is in the cache, it can be retrieved quickly without having to access the original data source. If the data is not in the cache, the system retrieves it from the original data source and stores a copy of the data in the cache for future access.

Caching can improve the performance and scalability of a system in several ways:

Reduced response time: Caching can significantly reduce the time required to access frequently accessed data by storing it in a high-speed cache. This can improve the overall performance of the system and reduce response times for users.

Reduced load on the original data source: By storing frequently accessed data in a cache, caching can reduce the load on the original data source. This can improve the scalability of the system by allowing it to handle more users or requests without becoming overwhelmed.

Improved availability: Caching can improve the availability of a system by reducing the likelihood of downtime or failures. If the original data source becomes unavailable, the system can still retrieve data from the cache, ensuring that the system remains operational.

Here is an example to illustrate the importance of caching in system design:

Suppose a company operates a website that provides real-time stock quotes to users. The website relies on an API to retrieve stock data from a third-party provider. Without caching, the website would need to retrieve stock data from the API every time a user requests a quote, which could result in slow response times and increased load on the API.

To improve performance and reduce the load on the API, the company might implement caching. The website could cache frequently accessed stock data in a high-speed storage system such as RAM or SSDs. When a user requests a quote, the system first checks the cache to see if the data is available. If the data is in the cache, it can be retrieved quickly without having to access the API. If the data is not in the cache, the system retrieves it from the API and stores a copy of the data in the cache for future access.

By implementing caching, the website can significantly improve the performance and scalability of the system by reducing the load on the API and improving response times for users.

In summary, caching is the process of storing frequently accessed data in a high-speed storage system in order to reduce the time and resources required to access that data from the original source. Caching is important in system design because it can significantly improve the performance and scalability of a system by reducing the load on the original data source and improving response times for users.

2.8   What is the CAP theorem? Can you provide a brief explanation of its three components?

The CAP theorem, also known as Brewer's theorem, is a principle in distributed systems that states that it is impossible for a distributed system to simultaneously provide all three of the following guarantees:

Consistency: Every read from the system returns the most recent write or an error.

Availability: Every request receives a response, without guarantee that it contains the most recent version of the information.

Partition tolerance: The system continues to operate even when network partitions occur.

The CAP theorem is often used as a framework for understanding the trade-offs involved in designing distributed systems. Let's take a closer look at each component of the CAP theorem:

Consistency: Consistency refers to the idea that every read from the system returns the most recent write or an error. In other words, if a user makes a change to the system, all subsequent reads from the system should reflect that change. Ensuring consistency requires that all nodes in the system have access to the same data and that any changes to the data are propagated to all nodes in a timely manner.

Availability: Availability refers to the idea that every request receives a response, without guarantee that it contains the most recent version of the information. In other words, the system is able to respond to user requests even if some nodes are unavailable or some data is temporarily unavailable. Ensuring availability requires that the system is designed to handle failures gracefully and that users are able to access the system even during periods of high load or network congestion.

Partition tolerance: Partition tolerance refers to the idea that the system continues to operate even when network partitions occur. In a distributed system, network partitions can occur when communication between nodes is disrupted, such as when a network link fails or a node goes down. Ensuring partition tolerance requires that the system is designed to handle network partitions gracefully, such as by using replication or other mechanisms to maintain data consistency even when nodes are isolated from each other.

Here is an example to illustrate the trade-offs involved in the CAP theorem:

Suppose a company is designing a distributed database system for managing customer orders. The company must choose between consistency, availability, and partition tolerance when designing the system.

If the company chooses consistency and partition tolerance, it may need to sacrifice availability in the event of a network partition. This means that users may not be able to access the system during a network outage.

If the company chooses availability and partition tolerance, it may need to sacrifice consistency, meaning that users may not always receive the most up-to-date information.

If the company chooses consistency and availability, it may need to sacrifice partition tolerance, meaning that the system may not be able to function during a network partition.

In summary, the CAP theorem states that it is impossible for a distributed system to simultaneously provide all three of consistency, availability, and partition tolerance. Designers of distributed systems must consider these trade-offs and make design decisions based on the specific requirements and constraints of their system.

2.9 Can you explain the difference between a monolithic architecture and a microservices architecture?

A monolithic architecture is a traditional approach to software design in which all components of an application are combined into a single, self-contained unit. In a monolithic architecture, all of the application's functionality is tightly coupled and runs as a single process on a single server. This means that any changes or updates to the application must be made to the entire codebase, and deploying a new version of the application requires deploying the entire monolith.

On the other hand, a microservices architecture is an approach to software design in which an application is broken down into a collection of small, loosely-coupled services that communicate with each other over a network. In a microservices architecture, each service is responsible for a specific task or set of tasks, and each service runs in its own process or container. This allows each service to be updated and deployed independently, without affecting the entire application.

The differences between a monolithic architecture and a microservices architecture can be summarized as follows:

Size and complexity: A monolithic architecture is typically larger and more complex than a microservices architecture, since all of the application's functionality is contained in a single codebase. A microservices architecture, on the other hand, is composed of smaller, more focused services that are easier to develop and maintain.

Coupling and dependencies: In a monolithic architecture, all of the application's functionality is tightly coupled, meaning that changes to one part of the application can have unintended effects on other parts of the application. In a microservices architecture, services are loosely coupled, meaning that changes to one service do not necessarily affect other services.

Scalability: A microservices architecture can be more scalable than a monolithic architecture, since individual services can be scaled independently based on their specific needs. In a monolithic architecture, scaling the entire application may be necessary, even if only certain parts of the application are experiencing high traffic.

Deployment and updates: A monolithic architecture requires deploying the entire codebase when making changes or updates to the application, while a microservices architecture allows individual services to be updated and deployed independently.

Here is an example to illustrate the differences between a monolithic architecture and a microservices architecture:

Suppose a company is developing an e-commerce website. In a monolithic architecture, the website would be developed as a single application, with all of the website's functionality contained in a single codebase. Any changes or updates to the website would require updating the entire monolith.

In a microservices architecture, the website would be developed as a collection of smaller, loosely-coupled services. For example, there might be a product catalog service, a shopping cart service, and a checkout service. Each service would be responsible for a specific set of tasks, and the services would communicate with each other over a network. This approach allows individual services to be updated and deployed independently, without affecting the entire website.

By using a microservices architecture, the company can achieve greater scalability, since individual services can be scaled independently based on their specific needs. The company can also update and deploy services more quickly and efficiently, since individual services can be updated without affecting the entire website.

In summary, a monolithic architecture is a traditional approach to software design in which all components of an application are combined into a single, self-contained unit, while a microservices architecture is an approach to software design in which an application is broken down into a collection of small, loosely-coupled services that communicate with each other over a network. The two architectures differ in terms of size and complexity, coupling and dependencies, scalability, and deployment and updates.

2.10 What is an API, and why is it important in system design?

An API, or Application Programming Interface, is a set of rules and protocols that defines how different software components should interact with each other. APIs are important in system design because they allow different software components to communicate and exchange information with each other, even if they were not originally designed to work together.

APIs can be thought of as a kind of interface between different software components. Just as a user interface allows users to interact with a software application, an API allows different software components to interact with each other. APIs define a set of rules and protocols for how different software components should communicate, such as by defining the data formats and methods that can be used to send and receive information.

APIs are important in system design for several reasons:

Encapsulation: APIs allow software components to encapsulate their functionality and data, making it easier to manage and maintain. By defining a clear interface, APIs allow software components to hide their internal implementation details, which can help to reduce complexity and improve modularity.

Interoperability: APIs allow different software components to work together even if they were not originally designed to work together. This can be particularly useful in large, complex systems where different components may have been developed by different teams or organizations.

Scalability: APIs can help to improve the scalability of a system by allowing different components to be deployed and scaled independently. By defining clear interfaces and protocols, APIs allow different components to communicate and exchange information in a consistent and reliable way.

Flexibility: APIs allow developers to experiment with new ideas and technologies without having to make major changes to existing software components. By defining a clear interface, APIs allow developers

to modify or replace individual components without affecting the rest
of the system.

Here is an example to illustrate the importance of APIs in system
design:

Suppose a company operates an e-commerce website that allows customers to purchase products online. The website uses a payment
processing system that was developed by a different company. In
order to integrate the payment processing system with the website,
the company could use an API provided by the payment processing
system.

The API would define a set of rules and protocols for how the website and the payment processing system should communicate, such as
by defining the data formats and methods that can be used to send
and receive payment information. By using the API, the company
can integrate the payment processing system with the website without having to develop their own payment processing system or make
major changes to the website.

In summary, an API is a set of rules and protocols that defines how
different software components should interact with each other. APIs
are important in system design because they allow different software
components to communicate and exchange information with each
other, even if they were not originally designed to work together.
APIs help to improve encapsulation, interoperability, scalability, and
flexibility, and are an essential part of modern software systems.

2.11   What is the role of a load balancer in a distributed system?

A load balancer is a component of a distributed system that distributes incoming network traffic across multiple servers or computing
resources in order to optimize resource utilization, increase availability, and improve performance. In other words, a load balancer helps
to distribute the load or workload of incoming requests to different
computing resources in a balanced and efficient way.

Load balancers are important in distributed systems for several reasons:

Scalability: Load balancers can help to improve the scalability of a distributed system by distributing incoming traffic across multiple servers or computing resources. This can help to ensure that the system is able to handle a large number of requests without becoming overwhelmed.

Availability: Load balancers can help to improve the availability of a distributed system by distributing incoming traffic across multiple servers or computing resources. If one server or resource becomes unavailable, the load balancer can redirect traffic to other available resources, helping to ensure that the system remains operational.

Performance: Load balancers can help to improve the performance of a distributed system by distributing incoming traffic across multiple servers or computing resources. This can help to reduce response times and improve the overall user experience.

Here is an example to illustrate the role of a load balancer in a distributed system:

Suppose a company operates a web application that allows users to search and book flights. The web application is hosted on multiple servers to ensure scalability and availability. A load balancer is used to distribute incoming traffic across the different servers.

When a user requests a flight search, the request is first sent to the load balancer. The load balancer then routes the request to one of the available servers based on predefined algorithms or rules. The load balancer may take into account factors such as server capacity, server availability, and geographic location when deciding which server to send the request to.

Once the request has been processed by the server, the response is sent back to the load balancer, which then forwards the response back to the user. If one of the servers becomes unavailable or is experiencing high traffic, the load balancer can redirect traffic to other available servers, helping to ensure that the system remains operational and responsive.

In summary, a load balancer is an important component of a distributed system that helps to distribute incoming network traffic across multiple servers or computing resources in order to improve scalability, availability, and performance. Load balancers are an essential part of modern distributed systems and play a critical role in ensuring that these systems remain efficient and reliable.

2.12   Can you differentiate between stateless and stateful systems?

Stateless and stateful systems are two different approaches to designing software applications, particularly in distributed systems. Let's take a closer look at each approach:

Stateless Systems: In a stateless system, each request or transaction is treated as an independent event, and the system does not maintain any state or memory of previous requests. In other words, each request is self-contained and does not depend on any previous requests or transactions. Stateless systems are often used in RESTful web services and APIs, where each HTTP request is treated as a separate transaction.

In a stateless system, all necessary information required to process a request is contained within the request itself. This means that each request is independent and can be processed by any available computing resource without requiring any additional context or state. Stateless systems are often easier to scale and maintain, since each request can be processed independently without affecting other requests or transactions.

Here is an example to illustrate a stateless system: Suppose a company operates a web service that provides weather forecasts for different locations around the world. The web service is designed as a stateless system, where each request for a weather forecast is treated as a separate, independent transaction. The web service does not maintain any state or memory of previous requests.

When a user requests a weather forecast for a particular location, the request is sent to the web service. The web service processes the request, retrieves the necessary information, and returns the weather forecast to the user. The web service does not maintain any information about the user or the previous requests, and each request is treated as an independent transaction.

Stateful Systems: In a stateful system, the system maintains a memory or state of previous requests or transactions. In other words, each request or transaction is dependent on the previous requests or transactions, and the system must maintain a context or state to ensure that each request is processed correctly. Stateful systems are often used in applications that require sessions, such as e-commerce websites or online banking systems.

In a stateful system, the system maintains information about the user and the previous requests or transactions. This information is used to ensure that each request is processed correctly and to provide a personalized experience for the user. Stateful systems are often more complex and difficult to scale than stateless systems, since the system must maintain information about the user and the previous requests or transactions.

Here is an example to illustrate a stateful system: Suppose a company operates an e-commerce website that allows users to browse and purchase products. The e-commerce website is designed as a stateful system, where each request is dependent on the previous requests and the system maintains a context or state.

When a user logs in to the website, the system maintains information about the user, such as the user's account details, shopping cart contents, and order history. Each request that the user makes, such as browsing products or making a purchase, depends on the previous requests and the user's context or state. The system uses this information to ensure that each request is processed correctly and to provide a personalized experience for the user.

In summary, stateless and stateful systems are two different approaches to designing software applications, particularly in distributed systems. Stateless systems treat each request as an independent event and do not maintain any memory of previous requests, while stateful systems maintain a context or state of previous requests and transactions. Stateless systems are often easier to scale and maintain, while stateful systems provide a more personalized and complex experience for the user.

2.13   What are the primary differences between synchronous and asynchronous communication in system design?

Synchronous and asynchronous communication are two different approaches to handling communication between different components in a distributed system. Let's take a closer look at each approach:

Synchronous Communication: In synchronous communication, the sender waits for a response from the receiver before proceeding with any further processing. In other words, the sender and receiver are in direct communication, and the sender cannot proceed until it receives a response from the receiver. Synchronous communication is often used in applications where immediate responses are required, such as real-time chat applications or online multiplayer games.

Here is an example to illustrate synchronous communication: Suppose a user requests a file from a server using a synchronous communication protocol. The user sends a request to the server, and the server waits for the request to be received before processing the request. Once the server processes the request, it sends a response back to the user, and the user waits for the response to be received before proceeding with any further processing.

Asynchronous Communication: In asynchronous communication, the sender does not wait for a response from the receiver before proceeding with any further processing. In other words, the sender and receiver are not in direct communication, and the sender can proceed with other tasks while waiting for a response from the receiver. Asynchronous communication is often used in applications where delayed responses are acceptable, such as email or message queues.

Here is an example to illustrate asynchronous communication: Suppose a user submits a job to a job queue using an asynchronous communication protocol. The user sends the job to the job queue and does not wait for a response from the job queue before proceeding with other tasks. The job queue receives the job and processes it, and the user can check the status of the job later to determine if it has completed.

The primary differences between synchronous and asynchronous communication can be summarized as follows:

Blocking vs Non-Blocking: Synchronous communication is blocking, meaning that the sender waits for a response from the receiver before proceeding with any further processing. Asynchronous communication is non-blocking, meaning that the sender can proceed with other tasks while waiting for a response from the receiver.

Latency vs Throughput: Synchronous communication is often used in applications where immediate responses are required, but it may not be suitable for applications that require high throughput or have high latency. Asynchronous communication is often used in applications where delayed responses are acceptable, and it can be used to improve throughput and reduce latency.

Complexity: Synchronous communication can be more complex than asynchronous communication, since it requires the sender and receiver to be in direct communication and to agree on a common protocol. Asynchronous communication can be simpler than synchronous communication, since it allows the sender and receiver to communicate without being in direct communication.

In summary, synchronous and asynchronous communication are two different approaches to handling communication between different components in a distributed system. Synchronous communication is blocking and often used in applications where immediate responses are required, while asynchronous communication is non-blocking and often used in applications where delayed responses are acceptable. The choice of communication approach depends on the specific requirements and constraints of the application.

2.14   What is data partitioning and why is it important in distributed systems?

Data partitioning, also known as sharding, is a technique used in distributed systems to divide large datasets into smaller, more manageable parts. Each part, or shard, is stored on a separate computing resource, allowing the system to scale horizontally and handle larger volumes of data.

Data partitioning is important in distributed systems for several reasons:

Scalability: By partitioning data into smaller parts, distributed systems can scale horizontally by adding additional computing resources to handle the increased load. This can help to improve performance and reduce the likelihood of data bottlenecks.

Availability: Data partitioning can help to improve the availability of a distributed system by reducing the impact of individual computing resource failures. If one computing resource fails, the remaining computing resources can continue to operate and serve data from the available shards.

Performance: Data partitioning can help to improve the performance of a distributed system by reducing the amount of data that needs to be processed in each request. By storing data on separate computing resources, requests can be processed in parallel, improving response times and reducing latency.

Here is an example to illustrate the importance of data partitioning in distributed systems:

Suppose a company operates a social media platform that allows users to post messages and interact with each other. The platform stores all user messages in a centralized database, which is becoming increasingly difficult to scale as the user base grows.

To address this issue, the company decides to implement data partitioning. They divide the database into smaller shards, each containing a subset of user messages. Each shard is stored on a separate computing resource, and the system uses a load balancer to distribute incoming requests across the different shards.

With data partitioning in place, the social media platform is now able to scale horizontally by adding additional computing resources to handle the increased load. Requests can be processed in parallel across the different shards, improving performance and reducing response times. In the event of a computing resource failure, the remaining computing resources can continue to operate and serve data from the available shards, improving availability.

In summary, data partitioning is a technique used in distributed systems to divide large datasets into smaller, more manageable parts. Data partitioning helps to improve scalability, availability, and performance by allowing the system to scale horizontally, reducing the impact of individual computing resource failures, and allowing requests to be processed in parallel. Data partitioning is an important concept in distributed systems and is essential for building scalable and reliable systems.

2.15 What are some common data storage options (e.g., SQL, NoSQL) and their differences?

There are two main categories of data storage options: SQL (relational databases) and NoSQL (non-relational databases). Let's take a closer look at each category and their differences:

SQL (Relational Databases): SQL databases store data in tables with a pre-defined schema, where each table represents a specific type of entity and each row represents an instance of that entity. SQL databases enforce a rigid structure and rules to ensure data consistency and integrity. Some examples of SQL databases include MySQL, PostgreSQL, and Oracle.

The main advantages of SQL databases are:

ACID Compliance: SQL databases are ACID compliant, meaning they ensure that transactions are processed in a reliable and consistent manner, and that data is always in a valid state.

Strong Data Consistency: SQL databases enforce strict rules and constraints to ensure data consistency and integrity.

Mature Technology: SQL databases have been in use for decades and have a mature ecosystem of tools and technologies to support them.

However, the main disadvantages of SQL databases are:

Limited Scalability: SQL databases can become a bottleneck when handling large volumes of data or high traffic, and can be difficult to scale horizontally.

Schema Changes: Changing the schema of an SQL database can be difficult and time-consuming, and can require downtime or data migration.

NoSQL (Non-Relational Databases): NoSQL databases store data in a flexible, document-oriented format, where each document can have a different structure and fields. NoSQL databases are designed to handle large volumes of unstructured or semi-structured data and can be easier to scale horizontally than SQL databases. Some examples of NoSQL databases include MongoDB, Cassandra, and Amazon DynamoDB.

The main advantages of NoSQL databases are:

Scalability: NoSQL databases are designed to handle large volumes of data and can be scaled horizontally with relative ease.

Flexible Schema: NoSQL databases do not have a rigid schema, allowing for more flexibility and adaptability to changing data structures.

High Availability: NoSQL databases are designed to be highly available, with built-in replication and distribution features to ensure that data is always accessible.

However, the main disadvantages of NoSQL databases are:

Eventual Consistency: NoSQL databases may sacrifice strong data consistency in favor of availability and scalability, meaning that data may not always be immediately consistent across all nodes.

Learning Curve: NoSQL databases can be more complex to use and require specialized knowledge to set up and manage.

Lack of Maturity: NoSQL databases are a relatively new technology, and may not have the same level of maturity and support as SQL databases.

In summary, SQL and NoSQL databases are two main categories of data storage options. SQL databases enforce a rigid structure and rules to ensure data consistency and integrity, while NoSQL databases are designed to handle large volumes of unstructured or semi-structured data and can be easier to scale horizontally. The choice of database type depends on the specific needs and constraints of the application.

2.16 Can you provide a brief explanation of the client-server model?

The client-server model is a common architectural pattern used in computer networking and distributed systems. In this model, the system is divided into two main components: the client, which sends requests to the server, and the server, which processes the requests and returns a response to the client.

Here is a brief overview of the client-server model:

Client: The client is the component of the system that initiates requests to the server. Clients can be any device or software application that communicates with the server, such as a web browser, mobile app, or desktop application.

Server: The server is the component of the system that receives requests from the client, processes them, and returns a response. Servers can be any computing resource that is capable of processing requests, such as a web server, application server, or database server.

Request: The request is a message sent by the client to the server, containing information about the operation to be performed. Requests can take many forms, depending on the protocol and application being used.

Response: The response is a message sent by the server to the client, containing the result of the operation requested in the initial request. Responses can take many forms, such as HTML pages, JSON objects, or binary data.

The client-server model is used in many different types of applications and systems, such as web applications, online gaming, and database management systems. It is a flexible and scalable architecture that allows for distributed processing of requests and can be used to handle large volumes of traffic.

Here is an example to illustrate the client-server model:

Suppose a user visits a website using their web browser. The web browser acts as the client, sending a request to the web server for a specific web page. The web server processes the request, retrieves the necessary data from a database, and generates an HTML response containing the requested web page. The server sends the response back to the client, which displays the web page in the user's web browser.

In summary, the client-server model is a common architectural pattern used in computer networking and distributed systems. It consists of two main components: the client, which sends requests to the server, and the server, which processes the requests and returns a response. The client-server model is used in many different types of applications and systems and is a flexible and scalable architecture that allows for distributed processing of requests.

2.17   What is eventual consistency, and why is it important in distributed systems?

Eventual consistency is a concept used in distributed systems to describe a state where all replicas of a data store will eventually be consistent, but not necessarily immediately consistent. In other words, changes made to a data store are propagated asynchronously across different nodes in the system, and it may take some time for all nodes to become consistent.

The importance of eventual consistency in distributed systems lies in its ability to provide high availability and fault tolerance while still maintaining reasonable levels of data consistency. Eventual consistency allows for distributed systems to continue functioning even in the event of network partitions, node failures, and other types of failures.

Here is an example to illustrate eventual consistency in a distributed system:

Suppose a company operates an e-commerce website that allows customers to place orders for products. The website uses a distributed database to store order information, with multiple replicas located in different data centers around the world.

When a customer places an order, the order information is stored in the local replica of the database. The order information is then propagated asynchronously to other replicas in the system, with each replica eventually becoming consistent with the others.

During the propagation process, there may be situations where different replicas have different versions of the same data. For example, if a network partition occurs, some replicas may not receive the latest updates and may be out of sync with the rest of the system.

In an eventually consistent system, these inconsistencies are resolved over time as updates are propagated across the system. The system may use techniques such as conflict resolution and quorums to resolve inconsistencies and ensure that all replicas eventually become consistent.

The benefits of eventual consistency in a distributed system are:

High Availability: Eventual consistency allows the system to continue functioning even in the event of network partitions, node failures, and other types of failures.

Fault Tolerance: Eventual consistency allows the system to recover from failures and continue functioning even if some nodes are temporarily unavailable or in an inconsistent state.

Scalability: Eventual consistency allows the system to scale horizontally by adding additional nodes to the system without sacrificing consistency or availability.

However, the drawbacks of eventual consistency are:

Reduced Data Consistency: Eventual consistency sacrifices immediate data consistency in favor of availability and fault tolerance, meaning that data may not always be immediately consistent across all nodes.

Increased Complexity: Eventual consistency can be more complex to implement and manage than strong consistency, requiring specialized knowledge and tools to ensure data integrity and consistency.

In summary, eventual consistency is a concept used in distributed systems to describe a state where all replicas of a data store will eventually be consistent, but not necessarily immediately consistent. Eventual consistency is important in distributed systems because it provides high availability and fault tolerance while still maintaining reasonable levels of data consistency. However, eventual consistency sacrifices immediate data consistency in favor of availability and fault tolerance, and can be more complex to implement and manage than strong consistency.

2.18   What is a message queue, and what role does it play in system design?

A message queue is a common architectural pattern used in system design that enables asynchronous communication between different components of a distributed system. In a message queue system, messages are sent and received asynchronously between different components, with the message queue acting as a buffer and intermediary between the sender and receiver.

Here is a brief overview of how message queues work in system design:

Sender: The sender component of the system creates a message and sends it to the message queue. The message can be any type of data, such as text, binary, or JSON.

Message Queue: The message queue acts as a buffer and intermediary between the sender and receiver. It stores the message until the receiver is ready to receive it.

Receiver: The receiver component of the system retrieves the message from the message queue and processes it. The receiver can be any type of component, such as an application, a microservice, or a server.

The use of a message queue in system design can provide several benefits, including:

Asynchronous Communication: Message queues enable asynchronous communication between different components of a distributed system. This can help to improve system performance and scalability by reducing the need for synchronous communication.

Decoupling: Message queues can help to decouple different components of a system, allowing them to operate independently and reducing the risk of system failures or bottlenecks.

Load Balancing: Message queues can help to balance the load on different components of a system, distributing incoming requests evenly and reducing the risk of overloading any individual component.

Resiliency: Message queues can help to improve the resiliency of a system by providing a buffer and intermediary for messages. In the event of failures or downtime, messages can be stored in the queue until the system is restored.

Here is an example to illustrate the role of message queues in system design:

Suppose a company operates an e-commerce website that receives a large volume of orders every day. The website uses a message queue to process incoming orders, with a microservice responsible for retrieving and processing orders from the queue.

When a customer places an order on the website, the order information is sent to the message queue. The microservice responsible for processing orders retrieves the order information from the queue and processes it, updating inventory levels and sending confirmation emails to customers.

The use of a message queue in this scenario helps to decouple the different components of the system and improve its scalability and resiliency. Incoming orders can be processed asynchronously, reducing the need for synchronous communication and improving system performance. In the event of downtime or system failures, incoming orders can be stored in the message queue until the system is restored.

In summary, a message queue is a common architectural pattern used in system design that enables asynchronous communication between different components of a distributed system. Message queues can provide several benefits, including asynchronous communication, decoupling, load balancing, and resiliency. The use of a message queue can help to improve the performance, scalability, and resiliency of a distributed system.

2.19 Can you briefly explain the concept of a content delivery network (CDN) and its importance in system design?

A content delivery network (CDN) is a distributed system of servers that deliver web content to users based on their geographic location. CDNs are designed to improve the speed and reliability of content delivery by reducing latency and network congestion.

Here is a brief overview of how CDNs work in system design:

Content: The content to be delivered can be any type of web content, such as images, videos, or static HTML pages.

CDN Servers: The CDN consists of a network of servers located in different geographic regions. Each server stores a copy of the content to be delivered.

User Request: When a user requests content from the website, the request is routed to the nearest CDN server based on the user's geographic location.

Content Delivery: The CDN server delivers the content to the user, reducing latency and network congestion and improving the speed and reliability of content delivery.

The use of a CDN in system design can provide several benefits, including:

Improved Performance: CDNs can improve the speed and performance of content delivery by reducing latency and network congestion. By storing copies of content in multiple geographic locations, CDNs can deliver content to users more quickly and reliably.

Scalability: CDNs can help to improve the scalability of a system by reducing the load on origin servers. By caching content in CDN servers, CDNs can reduce the number of requests that need to be handled by the origin server.

Geographic Reach: CDNs can help to improve the geographic reach of a system by delivering content to users in different regions around the world. This can help to improve the user experience and expand the audience for the website or application.

Security: CDNs can provide security benefits by protecting against DDoS attacks and other types of network-based attacks. CDNs can also provide encryption and authentication features to improve the security of content delivery.

Here is an example to illustrate the importance of CDNs in system design:

Suppose a company operates a news website that receives a large volume of traffic from users around the world. The website uses a CDN to deliver news articles, images, and videos to users, with CDN servers located in multiple geographic regions.

When a user requests content from the website, the request is routed to the nearest CDN server based on the user's geographic location. The CDN server delivers the content to the user, reducing latency and network congestion and improving the speed and reliability of content delivery.

The use of a CDN in this scenario helps to improve the performance and scalability of the website, reduce the load on origin servers, and improve the user experience for users around the world.

In summary, a content delivery network (CDN) is a distributed system of servers that deliver web content to users based on their geographic location. CDNs can improve the performance, scalability, and security of content delivery, and are an important component of system design for websites and applications that receive a large volume of traffic from users around the world.

2.20 What is fault tolerance, and why is it important in system design?

Fault tolerance is the ability of a system to continue functioning even in the presence of hardware or software failures. In other words, a fault-tolerant system is designed to be able to detect and recover from failures without interrupting the overall operation of the system.

The importance of fault tolerance in system design lies in its ability to improve system reliability and availability. By designing a system to be fault-tolerant, the system can continue functioning even in the presence of hardware or software failures, reducing downtime and ensuring that critical services and applications remain available to users.

Here are some common techniques used to achieve fault tolerance in system design:

Redundancy: One common technique for achieving fault tolerance is redundancy. This involves duplicating critical components or services to ensure that there is always a backup available in the event of a failure. For example, a redundant server can be used to host a backup copy of critical data, ensuring that the data remains available even if the primary server fails.

Failover: Another technique for achieving fault tolerance is failover. This involves detecting a failure in one component of a system and automatically switching to a backup component to continue operation. For example, if a web server fails, a failover mechanism can automatically switch to a backup web server to continue serving requests.

Load Balancing: Load balancing is another technique that can be used to achieve fault tolerance by distributing requests across multiple servers or components. If one server fails, the load can be automatically redistributed to other servers to ensure that the system continues functioning.

Monitoring: Monitoring is an important aspect of achieving fault tolerance in system design. By monitoring the health and performance of system components, potential failures can be detected early, and preventative measures can be taken to avoid downtime.

Here is an example to illustrate the importance of fault tolerance in system design:

Suppose a company operates an online banking system that allows customers to perform financial transactions such as deposits, withdrawals, and transfers. The system uses a fault-tolerant design that includes redundant servers, failover mechanisms, and load balancing.

In the event of a hardware or software failure, the system is designed to automatically switch to a backup server or component to continue processing transactions. This ensures that critical financial services remain available to customers, even in the presence of failures.

The use of a fault-tolerant design in this scenario helps to improve the reliability and availability of the online banking system, reducing the risk of downtime and ensuring that customers can access critical financial services at all times.

In summary, fault tolerance is the ability of a system to continue functioning even in the presence of hardware or software failures. Fault tolerance is important in system design because it improves system reliability and availability, reducing downtime and ensuring that critical services and applications remain available to users. Common techniques used to achieve fault tolerance include redundancy, failover, load balancing, and monitoring.

Chapter 3

Intermediate

3.1 Can you explain the concept of sharding in a database and its benefits?

Sharding is a technique used in database design to horizontally partition data across multiple servers or nodes. In a sharded database, data is divided into smaller subsets called shards, which are distributed across multiple servers. Sharding can provide several benefits for large-scale database systems, including improved scalability, performance, and availability.

Here is a brief overview of how sharding works in database design:

Data Partitioning: The first step in sharding a database is to partition the data into smaller subsets called shards. Shards can be divided based on a variety of criteria, such as geographic location, customer segment, or date range.

Node Assignment: Once the data is partitioned into shards, each shard is assigned to a specific node or server in the sharded database system.

Query Routing: When a user submits a query to the sharded database, the query is routed to the appropriate node or server based on the location of the data being queried.

Data Aggregation: If the query requires data from multiple shards, the results are aggregated and returned to the user.

The use of sharding in database design can provide several benefits, including:

Improved Scalability: Sharding can improve the scalability of a database system by distributing data across multiple nodes or servers. This allows the system to handle larger volumes of data and more complex queries.

Better Performance: Sharding can improve database performance by reducing the load on individual nodes or servers. By distributing data across multiple nodes, the system can process queries more quickly and efficiently.

Increased Availability: Sharding can increase the availability of a database system by reducing the risk of downtime or data loss. If one node or server fails, the remaining nodes can continue processing queries and serving data.

Cost Savings: Sharding can also provide cost savings by allowing organizations to use lower-cost hardware and software components, rather than investing in expensive, high-end hardware.

Here is an example to illustrate the benefits of sharding in database design:

Suppose a company operates a social media platform with a large user base that generates a large volume of data. The company uses a sharded database to handle the high volume of user-generated content.

In the sharded database, user data is partitioned into smaller subsets called shards, which are distributed across multiple nodes or servers. When a user submits a query, the query is routed to the appropriate node based on the location of the data being queried.

The use of sharding in this scenario helps to improve the scalability and performance of the social media platform, allowing the system to handle large volumes of user-generated content and complex queries.

Sharding also increases the availability of the system by reducing the risk of downtime or data loss in the event of a hardware or software failure.

In summary, sharding is a technique used in database design to horizontally partition data across multiple servers or nodes. Sharding can provide several benefits for large-scale database systems, including improved scalability, performance, availability, and cost savings.

3.2 What are the different types of database indexes, and how do they help in optimizing queries?

In database design, an index is a data structure that is used to improve the performance of queries by providing a faster way to access data. Indexes are created on one or more columns of a table and can be used to optimize queries that filter, sort, or join data. There are several types of database indexes, each with its own advantages and disadvantages.

Here are some of the most common types of database indexes:

B-Tree Indexes: B-Tree indexes are the most common type of database index and are used to improve the performance of queries that filter data based on a single column. B-Tree indexes organize data in a tree-like structure, allowing for fast access to data based on the indexed column. B-Tree indexes are well-suited for queries that use equality or range conditions.

Bitmap Indexes: Bitmap indexes are used to improve the performance of queries that filter data based on multiple columns. Bitmap indexes create a bitmap for each possible combination of values for the indexed columns, allowing for fast access to data based on the indexed columns. Bitmap indexes are well-suited for queries that use multiple equality conditions.

Hash Indexes: Hash indexes are used to improve the performance of queries that filter data based on equality conditions. Hash indexes use a hash function to map each possible value of the indexed column to a unique location in the index, allowing for fast access to data based on the indexed column. Hash indexes are well-suited for queries that use equality conditions but are not well-suited for range conditions.

Full-Text Indexes: Full-text indexes are used to improve the performance of queries that search for text-based data, such as documents or web pages. Full-text indexes allow for fast access to data based on keywords or phrases, and can be used to support advanced search features such as word proximity and fuzzy matching.

The use of indexes in database design can provide several benefits, including:

Improved Query Performance: Indexes can improve query performance by providing a faster way to access data. By creating indexes on commonly queried columns, the system can process queries more quickly and efficiently.

Faster Sorting and Grouping: Indexes can also improve the performance of sorting and grouping operations by providing a pre-sorted data structure that can be quickly accessed and processed.

Reduced Disk I/O: Indexes can reduce the amount of disk I/O required to process queries by allowing the system to access data more efficiently. This can help to reduce the overall system load and improve performance.

Here is an example to illustrate the benefits of indexes in database design:

Suppose a company operates an e-commerce website that sells a large number of products. The website uses a database to store information about products, including the product name, description, price, and category.

To improve query performance, the database is designed with indexes on the product name, price, and category columns. When a user searches for a product by name, price, or category, the query can be processed more quickly and efficiently using the corresponding index.

The use of indexes in this scenario helps to improve the performance of the e-commerce website, allowing users to quickly find and purchase products. By reducing the amount of disk I/O required to process queries, the system can handle a larger volume of queries and improve overall system scalability.

In summary, indexes are a data structure used to improve the performance of queries by providing a faster way to access data. There are several types of database indexes, each with its own advantages and disadvantages. The use of indexes in database design can provide several benefits, including improved query performance, faster sorting and grouping, and reduced disk I/O.

3.3   What are the four main components of a RESTful API?

RESTful APIs (Representational State Transfer APIs) are a common way to create web services that can be accessed over HTTP. RESTful APIs are designed to be simple and flexible, allowing developers to easily create and consume web services. There are four main components of a RESTful API, which are:

Resource: A resource is a piece of data that can be accessed or manipulated using the API. In RESTful API design, each resource is identified by a unique URL (Uniform Resource Locator). For example, a resource for a user profile might be identified by the URL "/users/user_id".

Verb: A verb is an HTTP method that is used to interact with a resource. The most commonly used HTTP verbs in RESTful API design are GET, POST, PUT, and DELETE. GET is used to retrieve data, POST is used to create new data, PUT is used to update existing data, and DELETE is used to delete data.

Representation: A representation is the format in which a resource is returned by the API. The most commonly used representations in RESTful API design are JSON (JavaScript Object Notation) and XML (Extensible Markup Language).

Hypermedia: Hypermedia is a set of links that are included in the representation of a resource. These links can be used to navigate between related resources, allowing the API to provide a rich and dynamic user experience. Hypermedia links are often expressed using the HATEOAS (Hypermedia as the Engine of Application State) principle.

Here is an example to illustrate the four main components of a RESTful API:

Suppose a company operates an e-commerce website that allows users to browse and purchase products. The website uses a RESTful API to provide access to product data and user information.

When a user visits the website, the API is used to retrieve product data, such as product descriptions and prices, and user information, such as account details and purchase history. The API uses the following four main components to provide access to this data:

Resource: The resources in the API include products, users, and orders. Each resource is identified by a unique URL, such as "/products/product_id" or "/users/user_id".

Verb: The API uses HTTP verbs to interact with resources. For example, a GET request might be used to retrieve product data, a POST request might be used to create a new order, and a PUT request might be used to update user account information.

Representation: The API returns data in JSON format, which is a common format for web services. The JSON representation of a product might include fields such as product name, price, and description.

Hypermedia: The API includes hypermedia links that allow users to navigate between related resources. For example, a product representation might include links to related products, and a user representation might include links to order history or account settings.

In summary, the four main components of a RESTful API are resource, verb, representation, and hypermedia. These components provide a simple and flexible way to create web services that can be accessed over HTTP, and are commonly used in modern web development.

3.4 What are some common design patterns used in system design? Can you give a brief overview of a few?

Design patterns are common solutions to recurring design problems that can be used to simplify the process of system design. Design patterns can be applied in a wide range of contexts, including software architecture, database design, and user interface design. Here are a few common design patterns used in system design:

Model-View-Controller (MVC) Pattern: The MVC pattern is a software architecture pattern that separates an application into three interconnected components: the model, the view, and the controller. The model represents the data and business logic of the application, the view represents the user interface, and the controller mediates between the two. The MVC pattern is commonly used in web development and can help to improve code organization and maintainability.

Singleton Pattern: The Singleton pattern is a creational design pattern that ensures that a class has only one instance, and provides a global point of access to that instance. The Singleton pattern is commonly used for resources that are expensive to create or that should be shared across multiple components of an application. For example, a database connection object might be implemented as a Singleton to ensure that only one connection is used throughout the application.

Observer Pattern: The Observer pattern is a behavioral design pattern that defines a one-to-many relationship between objects, where a change to one object results in updates to all dependent objects. The Observer pattern is commonly used for event-driven systems, such as user interface components or network communication. For example, a user interface component might observe changes to a data model and update its display accordingly.

Factory Pattern: The Factory pattern is a creational design pattern that provides an interface for creating objects, but allows subclasses to decide which class to instantiate. The Factory pattern is commonly used when an application needs to create objects that share a common interface, but where the specific implementation of that interface may vary. For example, a factory pattern might be used to create database connection objects, where different implementations might be used for different database vendors.

Decorator Pattern: The Decorator pattern is a structural design pattern that allows behavior to be added to an individual object, either statically or dynamically, without affecting the behavior of other objects from the same class. The Decorator pattern is commonly used to add functionality to objects in a flexible and modular way. For example, a user interface component might be decorated with additional behavior, such as validation or data formatting.

Here is an example to illustrate the use of a design pattern in system design:

Suppose a company is developing a mobile application that uses a database to store user data. To ensure that the application can handle a large volume of user requests, the company decides to use the Singleton pattern to manage database connections.

In the application, a database connection object is implemented as a Singleton, which ensures that only one connection is used throughout the application. The Singleton provides a global point of access to the database connection, which can be shared across multiple components of the application.

By using the Singleton pattern, the company can improve the performance and scalability of the mobile application by ensuring that database connections are managed efficiently and effectively. The use of the Singleton pattern also simplifies the code and reduces the risk of errors and inconsistencies in database access.

In summary, design patterns are common solutions to recurring design problems that can be used to simplify the process of system design. There are many different design patterns, each with its own advantages and disadvantages. Common design patterns used in system design include the MVC pattern, Singleton pattern, Observer pattern, Factory pattern, and Decorator pattern.

3.5 What are some strategies for designing systems that can handle high levels of traffic?

Designing systems that can handle high levels of traffic is critical for ensuring the reliability, scalability, and availability of web-based applications. Here are some strategies for designing systems that can handle high levels of traffic:

Use Load Balancers: Load balancing is a technique that distributes incoming network traffic across multiple servers to avoid overloading any one server. By using load balancers, web applications can handle large amounts of traffic without affecting performance or availability. Load balancers can be hardware-based or software-based, and can be configured to use different load-balancing algorithms depending on the specific requirements of the application.

Implement Caching: Caching is a technique that stores frequently accessed data in memory, reducing the need to fetch the data from the underlying data store. By implementing caching, web applications can reduce the load on databases and other data stores, improving performance and scalability. Caching can be implemented at different layers of the system, including the application layer, database layer, and network layer.

Use Content Delivery Networks (CDNs): CDNs are distributed networks of servers that cache and deliver content to users based on their geographic location. By using CDNs, web applications can reduce the load on their servers and improve performance for users located far away from the server. CDNs can be used to cache static content, such as images and videos, as well as dynamic content, such as web pages and API responses.

Implement Horizontal Scaling: Horizontal scaling is the process of adding more servers to a system to handle increased traffic. By adding more servers, web applications can distribute the load across multiple machines, improving performance and availability. Horizontal scaling can be implemented using techniques such as load balancing and auto-scaling, which automatically add or remove servers based on traffic levels.

Use Cloud-Based Infrastructure: Cloud-based infrastructure, such as Amazon Web Services (AWS) or Microsoft Azure, provides a scalable and flexible platform for building and deploying web applications. By using cloud-based infrastructure, web applications can take advantage of features such as auto-scaling, load balancing, and data replication, without having to manage the underlying infrastructure.

Here is an example to illustrate the use of these strategies in system design:

Suppose a company is developing an e-commerce website that needs to handle a large volume of traffic. To ensure that the website can handle high levels of traffic, the company decides to use the following strategies:

Use Load Balancers: The website is deployed on multiple servers, which are load-balanced using a software-based load balancer. The load balancer is configured to distribute traffic evenly across the servers, ensuring that no single server is overloaded.

Implement Caching: The website uses a caching layer to cache frequently accessed data, such as product information and user account data. The caching layer is implemented using a popular caching technology such as Redis or Memcached, which provides fast and efficient in-memory caching.

Use Content Delivery Networks (CDNs): The website uses a CDN to cache static content, such as images and videos, as well as dynamic content, such as web pages and API responses. The CDN is configured to cache content at edge locations close to the users, improving performance and reducing the load on the website servers.

Implement Horizontal Scaling: The website is designed to scale horizontally, with additional servers added as traffic levels increase. Auto-scaling is used to automatically add or remove servers based on traffic levels, ensuring that the website can handle sudden spikes in traffic without affecting performance.

Use Cloud-Based Infrastructure: The website is deployed on a cloud-based infrastructure such as AWS or Microsoft Azure, which provides a scalable and flexible platform for building and deploying web applications. The cloud-based infrastructure provides features such as auto-scaling, load balancing, and data replication, which are critical for ensuring the scalability

3.6 How do you deal with data consistency in distributed systems?

Maintaining data consistency is a critical challenge in distributed systems, where data is stored across multiple nodes and accessed by multiple clients simultaneously. Inconsistent data can lead to incorrect results, lost data, and reduced system reliability. Here are some strategies for dealing with data consistency in distributed systems:

Use a Consistency Model: A consistency model defines the level of consistency that a distributed system guarantees. There are several consistency models, including strong consistency, eventual consistency, and causal consistency. Strong consistency guarantees that all nodes in the system see the same data at the same time, while eventual consistency allows for temporary inconsistencies that are eventually resolved. Causal consistency ensures that the order of operations is maintained, even if different nodes see different data at different times. Choosing an appropriate consistency model depends on the specific requirements of the application.

Use a Distributed Database: Distributed databases are designed to provide consistent and reliable data access in a distributed system. Distributed databases can be implemented using techniques such as sharding, replication, and partitioning, which allow data to be distributed across multiple nodes while maintaining consistency. Distributed databases can also provide features such as transaction management and conflict resolution, which help to ensure data consistency.

Use Two-Phase Commit: Two-phase commit is a distributed transaction protocol that ensures that all nodes in a distributed system agree on the outcome of a transaction before it is committed. Two-phase commit involves two phases: the prepare phase, where all nodes are asked if they can commit the transaction, and the commit phase, where all nodes agree to commit the transaction. Two-phase commit is a reliable but slow protocol, and is typically used for critical transactions that require strong consistency.

Use Conflict Detection and Resolution: Conflict detection and resolution is a technique that detects conflicts between multiple clients
accessing the same data, and resolves those conflicts in a consistent
manner. Conflict detection and resolution can be implemented using
techniques such as timestamps, vector clocks, and last-writer-wins.
These techniques ensure that conflicting updates are handled in a
consistent manner, reducing the risk of data inconsistency.

Use Synchronization: Synchronization is a technique that ensures
that only one client can access a particular data item at a time, preventing conflicts and ensuring consistency. Synchronization can be
implemented using techniques such as locks, semaphores, and atomic
operations. These techniques ensure that conflicting updates are handled in a consistent manner, reducing the risk of data inconsistency.

Here is an example to illustrate the use of these strategies in system
design:

Suppose a company is developing a social media platform that allows users to create and share posts. To ensure that the platform
can handle a large volume of users and posts while maintaining data
consistency, the company decides to use the following strategies:

Use Eventual Consistency: The platform uses eventual consistency to
ensure that all nodes in the system eventually agree on the state of
the data. This allows for temporary inconsistencies that are eventually resolved, while still maintaining a high level of availability and
performance.

Use a Distributed Database: The platform uses a distributed database
to store user data and posts. The database is designed using techniques such as sharding and replication, which allow data to be distributed across multiple nodes while maintaining consistency.

Use Conflict Detection and Resolution: The platform uses conflict detection and resolution to handle conflicts between multiple users accessing the same data item. When a conflict is detected, the platform
uses a last-writer-wins approach to resolve the conflict in a consistent
manner.

Use Synchronization: The platform uses synchronization to ensure
that only one user can edit a particular post at a time. When a
user requests to edit a post, the platform acquires a lock on the post,

preventing other users from accessing it until the edit is complete.

By using these strategies, the company can ensure that the social media platform can handle

3.7 What is the role of a reverse proxy, and how does it differ from a load balancer?

A reverse proxy and a load balancer are both critical components of modern web applications. While they both help to distribute traffic across multiple servers, they have different roles and functions in system design. Here's a brief explanation of each:

Role of a Reverse Proxy: A reverse proxy is a server that sits between the client and the web server, forwarding requests from the client to the server and returning responses from the server to the client. A reverse proxy can be used for several purposes, including load balancing, caching, and security.

Load Balancing: A reverse proxy can be used to distribute traffic across multiple servers, improving performance and availability. The reverse proxy can be configured to use different load-balancing algorithms depending on the specific requirements of the application.

Caching: A reverse proxy can be used to cache frequently accessed content, such as static files and API responses. By caching content at the reverse proxy, the load on the web server can be reduced, improving performance and scalability.

Security: A reverse proxy can be used to provide an additional layer of security for web applications. By acting as a shield between the client and the web server, the reverse proxy can protect against attacks such as distributed denial of service (DDoS) and SQL injection.

Role of a Load Balancer: A load balancer is a server that sits between the client and the web servers, distributing traffic across multiple servers to avoid overloading any one server. Load balancers can be hardware-based or software-based, and can be configured to use different load-balancing algorithms depending on the specific requirements of the application.

Load Balancing: The primary role of a load balancer is to distribute traffic across multiple servers, improving performance and availability. Load balancers can use different load-balancing algorithms, such as round-robin, least connections, and IP hash, to ensure that traffic is distributed evenly across the servers.

Failover: Load balancers can also be configured to provide failover support, automatically redirecting traffic to healthy servers in the event of a server failure. This ensures that the application remains available even if one or more servers fail.

In summary, while both a reverse proxy and a load balancer can be used to distribute traffic across multiple servers, they have different roles and functions in system design. A reverse proxy can be used for load balancing, caching, and security, while a load balancer is primarily used for load balancing and failover.

3.8   What is idempotency in the context of system design, and why is it important?

Idempotency is a critical concept in system design that refers to the property of an operation or function where it can be applied multiple times, and the result will be the same as applying it only once. In other words, if the same operation is performed multiple times, it should produce the same result as if it were performed only once.

Idempotency is important in system design for several reasons:

Preventing unintended actions: In a distributed system, multiple requests can be sent to the same resource or service simultaneously. Without idempotency, a duplicate request can cause unintended actions or produce incorrect results, leading to data corruption or system failure.

Handling network errors: Idempotency can help in handling network errors, which are common in distributed systems. In case of a network error or timeout, the client can reattempt the request without worrying about producing unexpected results or modifying the system state.

Improving performance: Idempotency can also help in improving system performance by reducing the number of requests that need to be sent to the server. For example, if a client sends a request multiple times due to network errors or retry logic, idempotency ensures that the server only processes the request once, reducing the load on the server.

Here's an example to illustrate the importance of idempotency in system design:

Suppose a client application needs to update the quantity of a product in an e-commerce system. Without idempotency, if the client sends the same request multiple times, the system might update the quantity multiple times, leading to data inconsistency. However, if the update operation is designed to be idempotent, then the system would update the quantity only once, regardless of how many times the request was sent. This ensures that the system remains consistent and avoids unintended actions.

In conclusion, idempotency is an important concept in system design, particularly in distributed systems where multiple requests can be sent to the same resource or service simultaneously. By ensuring that operations are idempotent, we can prevent unintended actions, handle network errors, and improve system performance.

3.9 Can you explain the concept of a service-oriented architecture (SOA)?

Service-Oriented Architecture (SOA) is an architectural pattern that structures software applications as a collection of services. A service is a self-contained unit of functionality that can be accessed by other services or applications through a network or an application programming interface (API). The primary objective of SOA is to create a loosely coupled, modular, and scalable architecture that can integrate with other systems and adapt to changing business requirements.

Here are some key characteristics of SOA:

Services: The core building blocks of SOA are services, which are self-contained units of functionality that can be accessed through a network or an API. Services are designed to be modular, reusable, and interoperable, and can be developed using different technologies and platforms.

Loose Coupling: SOA promotes loose coupling between services, which means that services are designed to be independent of each other, with minimal dependencies between them. This allows services to be developed, deployed, and updated independently, without affecting other services or the overall system.

Interoperability: SOA emphasizes interoperability between different services and systems, allowing them to communicate and exchange data through standardized interfaces and protocols. This enables organizations to integrate different systems and services, even if they are developed using different technologies and platforms.

Scalability: SOA is designed to be scalable, allowing organizations to add or remove services as needed to meet changing business requirements. Services can be scaled horizontally (by adding more instances) or vertically (by increasing the capacity of individual instances) to handle increased traffic or workload.

Reusability: SOA promotes the reuse of services, which can reduce development time, improve system quality, and lower costs. Services can be designed to be modular and reusable, with standardized interfaces that can be accessed by different applications or services.

Here is an example to illustrate the concept of SOA:

Suppose a company has a web-based e-commerce platform that allows customers to purchase products online. The company decides to implement SOA to improve the scalability, flexibility, and interoperability of the system. The company breaks down the functionality of the platform into several services, including a product catalog service, a shopping cart service, a payment service, and a shipping service.

Each service is designed to be independent of the others, with minimal dependencies and a standardized interface that can be accessed by other services or applications. The services communicate and exchange data through a network or an API, allowing the system to be easily integrated with other systems or services. The company can add or remove services as needed to meet changing business requirements, and can scale the services horizontally or vertically to handle increased traffic or workload.

By using SOA, the company can create a modular, scalable, and interoperable architecture that can adapt to changing business requirements and integrate with other systems and services.

3.10 How do you ensure data durability in a distributed system?

Ensuring data durability in a distributed system is a critical aspect of system design. Data durability refers to the ability of a system to retain data even in the event of hardware or software failures. In a distributed system, achieving data durability can be challenging, as data is distributed across multiple nodes and can be subject to network failures, server failures, and other types of failures.

Here are some strategies for ensuring data durability in a distributed system:

Replication: One of the most common strategies for ensuring data durability is replication. Replication involves creating multiple copies of data and distributing them across different nodes in the system. If one node fails, another node can take over, ensuring that the data is still available. Replication can be synchronous (data is written to all replicas at the same time) or asynchronous (data is written to the primary node first and then replicated to the other nodes).

Redundancy: Redundancy involves duplicating the hardware and software components of the system to ensure that there is no single point of failure. Redundancy can be achieved at different levels, including network redundancy (using multiple network paths), server redundancy (using multiple servers), and storage redundancy (using multiple storage devices).

Data backups: Regular data backups can ensure that data can be restored in the event of a failure. Backups can be stored locally or in a separate location to ensure that they are not affected by a failure in the primary system. Backups can be performed at different intervals, depending on the criticality of the data and the frequency of changes.

Write-ahead logging: Write-ahead logging involves writing data to a log file before writing it to the database. This ensures that data changes are recorded in the log file, even if they are not immediately written to the database. If a failure occurs, the system can use the log file to recover the data.

Consistency models: Consistency models define how data consistency is maintained in a distributed system. Strong consistency models ensure that all nodes in the system have the same view of the data at all times, while weaker consistency models allow some degree of inconsistency. Choosing the right consistency model depends on the specific requirements of the system and the trade-offs between consistency, availability, and partition tolerance.

Here's an example to illustrate the importance of ensuring data durability in a distributed system:

Suppose a company has a distributed database that stores customer information for its e-commerce platform. To ensure data durability, the company implements replication, with multiple copies of the data distributed across different nodes in the system. The company also performs regular backups of the data, storing them in a separate location to ensure that they are not affected by a failure in the primary system.

To further improve data durability, the company implements a strong consistency model, ensuring that all nodes in the system have the same view of the data at all times. The company also uses write-ahead logging to record data changes before they are written to the database, ensuring that data can be recovered in the event of a failure.

By implementing these strategies, the company can ensure that customer data is durable and available, even in the event of hardware or software failures.

3.11 What are some common techniques for optimizing database performance?

Optimizing database performance is critical in any system that relies on a database to store and retrieve data. There are several techniques that can be used to improve database performance, including the following:

Indexing: Indexing involves creating indexes on database tables to speed up queries. An index is a data structure that allows the database to quickly locate data based on the values in one or more columns. By creating indexes on frequently queried columns, database performance can be improved significantly.

Partitioning: Partitioning involves splitting large database tables into smaller ones to improve query performance. Partitioning can be done based on various criteria, such as range partitioning (based on a range of values in a column), hash partitioning (based on a hash function), or list partitioning (based on a list of values in a column).

Query optimization: Query optimization involves analyzing database queries to identify opportunities to improve performance. This can be done by optimizing the query structure, using appropriate joins, avoiding subqueries, and reducing the number of columns returned.

Caching: Caching involves storing frequently accessed data in memory to speed up access times. This can be done at various levels, such as database-level caching (using a cache to store query results), application-level caching (storing frequently accessed data in the application), or client-side caching (storing data on the client side).

Connection pooling: Connection pooling involves reusing database connections to avoid the overhead of establishing new connections for each query. Connection pooling can improve performance by reducing the time required to establish a connection, especially in systems with high levels of traffic.

Here's an example to illustrate the importance of optimizing database performance:

Suppose a company has an e-commerce platform that relies on a database to store customer information, product information, and order data. The company experiences slow query performance, leading to slow page load times, high server load, and poor user experience.

To improve database performance, the company implements indexing on frequently queried columns, such as product ID and customer ID. The company also partitions large tables, such as the order table, based on range partitioning. The company optimizes database queries by reducing the number of subqueries and avoiding the use of temporary tables.

To further improve performance, the company implements caching at various levels, including database-level caching and application-level caching. The company also uses connection pooling to reuse database connections, reducing the overhead of establishing new connections.

By implementing these techniques, the company can significantly improve database performance, resulting in faster page load times, reduced server load, and improved user experience.

3.12   How do you handle bottlenecks in system design?

Bottlenecks can occur in any system design when a particular component or process becomes a limiting factor in overall system performance. In order to handle bottlenecks in system design, there are a number of strategies that can be employed, including the following:

Identifying the bottleneck: The first step in handling bottlenecks is identifying the root cause of the problem. This may involve monitoring system performance and analyzing logs to identify the component or process that is causing the bottleneck. Once the bottleneck has been identified, it is important to understand the factors that are contributing to it.

Scaling horizontally or vertically: One of the most common strategies for handling bottlenecks is scaling the system horizontally or vertically. Horizontal scaling involves adding more nodes or servers to the system to increase capacity. Vertical scaling involves increasing the resources (such as CPU or memory) on existing nodes or servers. Choosing the right scaling strategy depends on the nature of the bottleneck and the overall system design.

Optimizing code or queries: Bottlenecks can often be caused by inefficient code or queries. Optimizing code and queries can help to improve system performance and reduce the impact of bottlenecks. This may involve optimizing algorithms, reducing the number of database queries, or improving network performance.

Implementing caching: Caching involves storing frequently accessed data in memory to speed up access times. By implementing caching at various levels, such as database-level caching, application-level caching, or client-side caching, bottlenecks can be reduced and system performance can be improved.

Load balancing: Load balancing involves distributing traffic across multiple nodes or servers to improve performance and reduce the impact of bottlenecks. Load balancing can be done at different levels, such as network load balancing, server load balancing, or application load balancing.

Here's an example to illustrate how to handle bottlenecks in system design:

Suppose a company has an online store that experiences slow page load times during peak traffic periods. After monitoring system performance and analyzing logs, the company identifies a bottleneck in the database, specifically in the product table queries. The queries are slow due to the large number of rows in the table and the complexity of the queries.

To handle the bottleneck, the company decides to optimize the database queries by adding indexes on frequently accessed columns, reducing the number of joins, and optimizing the query structure. The company also implements database-level caching to store frequently accessed data in memory and reduce query times.

To further improve performance, the company decides to scale the system horizontally by adding more database nodes and implementing load balancing. The company also optimizes the application code by reducing the number of database queries and optimizing network performance.

By implementing these strategies, the company is able to handle the bottleneck in the database and improve system performance, resulting in faster page load times and improved user experience.

3.13   What is a publish-subscribe pattern, and how does it differ from a request-response pattern?

The publish-subscribe pattern and request-response pattern are two commonly used messaging patterns in system design. While they serve similar purposes, they differ in their approach and usage.

Publish-subscribe pattern: The publish-subscribe pattern is a messaging pattern where publishers send messages to a topic, and subscribers receive messages from the topic. In this pattern, publishers do not send messages directly to specific subscribers, but rather publish messages to a topic that subscribers can then receive.

The main advantage of the publish-subscribe pattern is that it allows for decoupling between publishers and subscribers. Publishers do not need to know who the subscribers are or how many of them there are, and subscribers do not need to know who the publishers are or how many of them there are. This allows for a highly scalable and flexible messaging system.

An example of the publish-subscribe pattern in action is a news website that publishes articles to different categories, such as sports, politics, and entertainment. Subscribers can choose which categories they are interested in and receive articles from those categories as they are published.

Request-response pattern: The request-response pattern is a messaging pattern where a client sends a request to a server and the server responds with a message. In this pattern, the client initiates the communication by sending a request, and the server responds to the request with a message.

The main advantage of the request-response pattern is that it allows for synchronous communication between the client and the server.

The client can wait for a response before proceeding, and the server can provide a response in a timely manner.

An example of the request-response pattern in action is a web application that sends a request to a database to retrieve data, and the database responds with the requested data.

Differences between the patterns: The main difference between the publish-subscribe pattern and the request-response pattern is that the publish-subscribe pattern is asynchronous, while the request-response pattern is synchronous. In the publish-subscribe pattern, messages are sent and received independently of each other, while in the request-response pattern, a response is required before the next action can be taken.

Another difference is that the publish-subscribe pattern allows for multiple subscribers to receive the same message, while the request-response pattern is a one-to-one communication between the client and server.

In summary, the publish-subscribe pattern and request-response pattern are two commonly used messaging patterns in system design. The publish-subscribe pattern is asynchronous and allows for decoupling between publishers and subscribers, while the request-response pattern is synchronous and involves a one-to-one communication between the client and server.

3.14   Can you explain the benefits and drawbacks of using a NoSQL database over a traditional SQL database?

NoSQL and SQL databases have different approaches to data storage and retrieval, and each has its own set of benefits and drawbacks. Here are some of the key differences:

Benefits of NoSQL databases:

Scalability: NoSQL databases are designed to be highly scalable and distributed, allowing them to handle large amounts of data and high traffic loads. They can be easily scaled horizontally by adding more servers or nodes.

Flexibility: NoSQL databases are schemaless, meaning that they can store data in any format without requiring a predefined schema. This allows for greater flexibility in data storage and retrieval.

Performance: NoSQL databases are optimized for performance, with fast read and write times and the ability to handle large volumes of data.

Availability: NoSQL databases are designed to be highly available, with built-in replication and fault-tolerance features that ensure data availability even in the event of hardware failures.

Drawbacks of NoSQL databases:

Limited query capabilities: NoSQL databases often have limited query capabilities compared to SQL databases, which can make complex data retrieval more difficult.

Lack of transactions: NoSQL databases may not support transactions, which can make it difficult to ensure data consistency in certain situations.

Less mature ecosystem: NoSQL databases are relatively new compared to SQL databases, which means that there may be fewer tools, resources, and community support available.

Benefits of SQL databases:

Powerful querying capabilities: SQL databases have powerful querying capabilities that allow for complex data retrieval and analysis.

Strong data consistency: SQL databases support transactions and enforce strong data consistency, which can ensure that data is accurate and reliable.

Mature ecosystem: SQL databases have been around for a long time and have a mature ecosystem with many tools, resources, and community support available.

Drawbacks of SQL databases:

Limited scalability: SQL databases can be difficult to scale horizontally, which can make it challenging to handle large amounts of data and high traffic loads.

Limited flexibility: SQL databases require a predefined schema, which can limit flexibility in data storage and retrieval.

Performance: SQL databases can be slower than NoSQL databases for certain types of applications, particularly those with high read and write loads.

In summary, the choice between NoSQL and SQL databases depends on the specific requirements of the system being designed. NoSQL databases are well-suited for applications that require scalability, flexibility, and high performance, while SQL databases are better for applications that require powerful querying capabilities and strong data consistency. It's also worth noting that hybrid solutions, such as using both SQL and NoSQL databases together, can be a viable option in some cases.

3.15 What is a session in the context of system design, and how can you manage session state?

In the context of system design, a session refers to a period of interaction between a user and a web application or service. During a session, the user performs a series of actions (such as browsing pages, making requests, or submitting data), and the web application or service stores information about the user's activity and state.

Managing session state is important because it allows the web application or service to maintain context and continuity across a series of user interactions. This means that the user can navigate through the application or service without losing their place or having to constantly re-enter information.

Here are some common strategies for managing session state:

Cookies: Cookies are small text files that are stored on the user's

computer and used to store session information. The web application
or service can read and write cookies to store information about the
user's session state, such as their login status, preferences, or shopping
cart contents.

URL-based session management: URL-based session management involves including a unique session ID in the URL for each page that
the user visits. The web application or service can use this session ID
to identify the user and maintain their session state.

Server-side session management: Server-side session management involves storing session information on the server, rather than on the
user's computer. When the user interacts with the web application
or service, the server retrieves and updates the session information as
necessary.

Distributed session management: Distributed session management involves storing session information across multiple servers, to improve
scalability and availability. In this approach, session information is
replicated across multiple servers, and load balancers are used to direct user requests to the appropriate server based on their session
ID.

It's important to note that managing session state can introduce security risks, such as session hijacking or cross-site scripting attacks. To
mitigate these risks, it's important to use secure session management
techniques, such as encrypting session data, using secure cookies, and
implementing measures to prevent session fixation attacks.

3.16 What are some key considerations when designing a system for high availability?

Designing a system for high availability involves ensuring that the
system can remain operational even in the face of hardware failures,
software errors, or other issues that could cause downtime or service
interruptions. Here are some key considerations when designing for
high availability:

Redundancy: Redundancy is the practice of creating backup copies of critical components of the system, such as servers, storage devices, and network connections. By creating redundant components, the system can continue to operate even if one or more components fail.

Load balancing: Load balancing involves distributing incoming requests across multiple servers or instances, to prevent any one server from becoming overloaded. Load balancing can help ensure that the system remains responsive and available even under heavy traffic loads.

Failover: Failover is the process of automatically switching to a backup system or component in the event of a failure. For example, if a server fails, a failover mechanism might automatically switch traffic to a redundant server to minimize downtime.

Monitoring and alerting: Monitoring and alerting tools can help ensure that the system remains available by detecting issues early and alerting system administrators before they become critical. Monitoring tools might track system metrics such as CPU usage, memory usage, and network traffic, while alerting tools might send notifications via email, SMS, or other means.

Disaster recovery: Disaster recovery involves creating plans and procedures for recovering from catastrophic events such as natural disasters, cyber attacks, or data center outages. Disaster recovery plans might include backup and restore procedures, data replication strategies, and failover mechanisms to ensure that the system can be quickly restored in the event of a major outage.

Testing and validation: Testing and validation are critical for ensuring that the system is designed to be highly available. This might include load testing to ensure that the system can handle heavy traffic loads, performance testing to ensure that the system remains responsive under stress, and failover testing to ensure that backup mechanisms are working as intended.

By considering these key factors when designing for high availability, system designers can create systems that are resilient, reliable, and able to withstand a wide range of challenges and failures.

3.17   Can you explain the concept of data replication in distributed systems and its importance?

Data replication is the process of creating copies of data and distributing them across multiple nodes or servers in a distributed system. The purpose of data replication is to improve system performance, increase fault tolerance, and ensure data availability.

In a distributed system, data may be replicated for several reasons, including:

Performance: By replicating data across multiple nodes, the system can reduce the amount of data that needs to be transferred between nodes, improving performance and reducing network traffic.

Availability: By replicating data across multiple nodes, the system can ensure that data is available even if one or more nodes fail or become unavailable.

Geographic distribution: By replicating data across multiple geographically distributed nodes, the system can improve response times for users in different locations and ensure that data is available even in the event of a natural disaster or other catastrophic event.

Consistency: By replicating data across multiple nodes, the system can ensure that all nodes have consistent and up-to-date copies of the data.

Data replication can be implemented in several ways, including:

Master-slave replication: In master-slave replication, one node (the master) is responsible for writing data, while one or more other nodes (the slaves) are responsible for reading data. When data is written to the master, it is automatically replicated to the slaves, ensuring that all nodes have consistent copies of the data.

Multi-master replication: In multi-master replication, multiple nodes are responsible for both reading and writing data. When data is written to one node, it is automatically replicated to the other nodes, ensuring that all nodes have consistent copies of the data.

Sharding: Sharding is a technique for distributing data across multiple nodes based on a defined partitioning scheme. Each node is responsible for a specific subset of the data, ensuring that the system can scale horizontally and handle large amounts of data.

Data replication is important in distributed systems because it helps ensure that data is available and consistent across the entire system, even in the event of hardware failures, network outages, or other issues. By replicating data across multiple nodes, the system can also improve performance, reduce network traffic, and ensure that data is available to users in different locations.

3.18 What is a circuit breaker pattern, and how does it help in improving the resilience of a system?

The circuit breaker pattern is a design pattern that helps improve the resilience of a system by detecting and handling failures in a graceful manner. The pattern is based on the concept of an electrical circuit breaker, which is designed to prevent damage to an electrical system in the event of a power surge or other overload.

In a software system, the circuit breaker pattern is typically used to detect failures in remote services or APIs that the system relies on, and to prevent cascading failures that could bring down the entire system. When a failure is detected, the circuit breaker trips and stops making requests to the failed service, instead returning a fallback response or error message. This allows the system to continue functioning, even if the failed service is not available.

The circuit breaker pattern typically includes three states:

Closed: In the closed state, the circuit breaker is allowing requests to pass through to the remote service. This is the normal operating state when the remote service is functioning correctly.

Open: In the open state, the circuit breaker has detected a failure in the remote service and is no longer allowing requests to pass through. Instead, it returns a fallback response or error message.

Half-open: In the half-open state, the circuit breaker allows a limited number of requests to pass through to the remote service, to determine whether it has recovered. If the requests are successful, the circuit breaker returns to the closed state. If the requests fail, it returns to the open state.

The circuit breaker pattern can improve the resilience of a system in several ways. First, by detecting failures and preventing cascading failures, it helps ensure that the system remains operational even if one or more components fail. Second, by returning a fallback response or error message, it helps ensure that users are not left waiting for long periods of time or experiencing errors. Finally, by allowing the system to continue functioning even when a remote service is unavailable, it helps ensure that the system can scale horizontally and handle large amounts of traffic.

Example:

Let's consider an e-commerce application that relies on a payment gateway service to process payments. If the payment gateway service experiences a failure or is overwhelmed with traffic, it could cause the entire application to become unresponsive, resulting in lost sales and dissatisfied customers.

By using the circuit breaker pattern, the e-commerce application can detect when the payment gateway service is unavailable and stop making requests to it. Instead, it can return a fallback response or error message to the user, such as a message that the payment service is currently unavailable and to try again later. This helps ensure that the user is not left waiting for long periods of time or experiencing errors, and that the application remains operational even in the event of a payment gateway failure.

3.19 What are the key factors to consider when choosing between synchronous and asynchronous communication in a system?

When designing a system, it's important to choose the right communication protocol to ensure that it can handle the workload and meet the performance requirements. Two common communication protocols used in systems are synchronous and asynchronous communication.

Synchronous communication involves sending a request and waiting for a response before proceeding with the next task. In other words, the client blocks and waits for the server to respond. Asynchronous communication, on the other hand, involves sending a request and continuing with other tasks while waiting for a response. The client does not block and can continue processing other requests while waiting for the response.

There are several key factors to consider when choosing between synchronous and asynchronous communication:

Performance: Synchronous communication can be faster and more efficient for small requests and low-latency systems, as it reduces the overhead associated with managing multiple requests and responses. Asynchronous communication can be more efficient for larger requests and high-latency systems, as it allows the client to continue processing other requests while waiting for a response.

Scalability: Asynchronous communication can be more scalable, as it allows the system to handle a larger number of requests without becoming blocked or overwhelmed. Synchronous communication can be less scalable, as it can become blocked if too many requests are made at once.

Complexity: Asynchronous communication can be more complex to implement, as it requires additional infrastructure to manage requests and responses. Synchronous communication can be simpler to implement, as it does not require this additional infrastructure.

Error handling: Asynchronous communication can be more resilient to errors, as it allows the system to continue processing other requests even if one request fails. Synchronous communication can be less resilient to errors, as a failed request can block the system and prevent other requests from being processed.

User experience: Synchronous communication can provide a better user experience for tasks that require immediate feedback, such as form submissions or login requests. Asynchronous communication can provide a better user experience for tasks that take longer to complete, such as uploading a large file or processing a batch job.

Example:

Consider a social media platform that allows users to post updates and comment on other users' posts. When a user posts an update, the system must notify all of the user's followers about the update.

Synchronous communication could be used to notify each follower individually, blocking the system until each notification is sent and confirmed. This could result in a slow and unresponsive system if the user has a large number of followers.

Asynchronous communication could be used to send notifications in the background, allowing the system to continue processing other requests while the notifications are being sent. This would allow the system to handle a large number of followers without becoming blocked or overwhelmed.

In this case, asynchronous communication would be a better choice, as it would allow the system to handle a large number of followers while remaining responsive and scalable.

3.20 Can you discuss the importance of monitoring and logging in a well-designed system?

Monitoring and logging are critical components of a well-designed system, as they provide visibility into the system's performance and help ensure that it is operating as expected.

Monitoring involves collecting and analyzing metrics about the system, such as CPU usage, memory usage, and network traffic. This allows system administrators to identify potential issues before they become critical, and to optimize the system's performance over time. Monitoring can also help identify trends and patterns in system usage, which can inform future design decisions.

Logging involves recording events and transactions that occur within the system, such as user actions, error messages, and system warnings. This provides a historical record of what has occurred within the system, which can be useful for troubleshooting issues, auditing user behavior, and identifying potential security threats.

There are several key benefits to monitoring and logging in a well-designed system:

Early detection of issues: Monitoring allows system administrators to detect issues before they become critical, such as spikes in traffic or resource usage. This can help prevent system downtime or failures.

Performance optimization: Monitoring can provide insights into the system's performance, allowing administrators to identify bottlenecks or areas that can be optimized for better performance.

Improved reliability: Logging can help identify errors or warning messages that may indicate potential reliability issues within the system. By identifying and addressing these issues, system reliability can be improved.

Security: Logging can be used to monitor user activity and detect potential security threats or breaches. It can also provide an audit trail for compliance and regulatory purposes.

Capacity planning: Monitoring can provide insights into system usage patterns, allowing administrators to plan for future capacity needs and make informed decisions about system scaling.

Example:

Consider an e-commerce website that experiences a sudden spike in traffic during a holiday season sale. Without monitoring, the system administrators may not be aware of the spike in traffic until it causes the system to become overwhelmed and crash. However, with monitoring in place, the administrators can detect the spike in traffic early and take steps to optimize the system's performance, such as adding additional servers or increasing the system's capacity.

In another example, a user reports an issue with the system, but is unable to provide specific details about what happened. Without logging, the system administrators may not be able to identify the cause of the issue and address it. However, with logging in place, the administrators can review the system's logs to identify the specific error or issue that occurred, and take steps to prevent it from happening again in the future.

Overall, monitoring and logging are essential components of a well-designed system, as they provide visibility and insights into the system's performance, reliability, and security. By implementing monitoring and logging, system administrators can proactively detect issues, optimize performance, and ensure that the system is operating as expected.

Chapter 4

Advanced

4.1 Can you discuss the concept of backpressure in system design and how it can be managed?

Backpressure is a critical concept in system design that refers to the ability of a system to handle and manage incoming requests or data when the system is under heavy load. Backpressure occurs when the system is unable to process incoming requests or data as quickly as they are being received, leading to a backlog of requests or data that need to be processed.

Managing backpressure is essential for ensuring that a system remains responsive and available, even under heavy load. There are several techniques for managing backpressure in a system, including:

Queueing: Incoming requests or data can be placed in a queue to be processed in the order they are received. This allows the system to handle incoming requests or data at its own pace, while still ensuring that they are processed in a timely manner.

Throttling: Throttling involves limiting the rate at which incoming requests or data are processed, to prevent the system from becoming overwhelmed. Throttling can be implemented in various ways, such as limiting the number of requests that can be processed at once or introducing a delay between requests.

Load shedding: Load shedding involves selectively dropping or discarding incoming requests or data that are deemed less important or lower priority. This allows the system to focus on processing the most important requests or data, while still maintaining overall performance and availability.

Scaling: Scaling involves adding additional resources, such as servers or processing power, to the system in order to handle increased load. This can be done manually or automatically, depending on the system's requirements.

Example:

Consider a real-time messaging system that allows users to send messages to each other in real-time. When the system is under heavy load, such as during a large-scale event, it may be unable to handle the incoming messages as quickly as they are being sent. If backpressure is not managed properly, this can lead to a backlog of messages that need to be processed, causing delays and potentially impacting the system's performance.

To manage backpressure in this scenario, the system could implement queueing, by placing incoming messages in a queue to be processed in the order they are received. The system could also implement throttling, by limiting the rate at which messages are processed to prevent the system from becoming overwhelmed. Additionally, the system could scale by adding additional resources, such as servers or processing power, to handle increased load.

By implementing these backpressure management techniques, the messaging system can maintain overall performance and availability, even under heavy load.

4.2 How do you handle schema changes and migrations in a distributed database system?

Schema changes and migrations can be challenging in distributed database systems, as they require careful coordination and management to ensure that data remains consistent across all nodes in the system. Here are some common techniques for handling schema changes and migrations in a distributed database system:

Blue-green deployment: One approach to managing schema changes and migrations in a distributed database system is to use a blue-green deployment strategy. In this approach, a new version of the schema is deployed to a separate set of nodes (the "green" nodes) while the existing nodes continue to run the old schema (the "blue" nodes). Once the new nodes are up and running, traffic can be gradually shifted over to the green nodes. If any issues arise during the migration, traffic can be redirected back to the blue nodes until the issues are resolved.

Rolling updates: Another approach is to use rolling updates, where the new schema is deployed to nodes in a phased approach, with a small number of nodes being updated at a time. This allows for gradual testing and validation of the new schema, while minimizing the risk of downtime or data inconsistencies.

Automated schema migrations: Automated schema migration tools can be used to help automate the process of deploying schema changes and migrations in a distributed database system. These tools can help ensure that the schema changes are applied consistently across all nodes in the system, while minimizing the risk of errors or data inconsistencies.

Versioning: It can be helpful to version the schema and keep a record of all changes and migrations that have been made. This can help ensure that all nodes in the system are running the correct version of the schema, and can provide a historical record of all changes that have been made to the system.

Example:

Consider a distributed database system that stores user data for a social networking application. If the application needs to add a new field to the user profile, such as a "bio" field, this will require a schema change and migration across all nodes in the system. To manage this change, the system could use a blue-green deployment approach, where the new schema is deployed to a separate set of nodes, and traffic is gradually shifted over to the new nodes. Alternatively, the system could use rolling updates, where the new schema is deployed to a small number of nodes at a time, and validated before rolling out to additional nodes.

Automated schema migration tools can also be used to help manage the deployment of schema changes and migrations. These tools can help ensure that the schema changes are applied consistently across all nodes in the system, while minimizing the risk of errors or data inconsistencies.

Overall, managing schema changes and migrations in a distributed database system requires careful coordination and planning to ensure that data remains consistent across all nodes in the system. By using appropriate deployment strategies and automated tools, these changes can be managed efficiently and effectively, while minimizing the risk of downtime or data inconsistencies.

4.3 What are some strategies for implementing rate limiting in a system?

Rate limiting is an important technique for managing traffic and preventing overload in a system. Here are some common strategies for implementing rate limiting in a system:

Token bucket algorithm: One approach to rate limiting is to use a token bucket algorithm. In this approach, a fixed number of tokens are generated at a set rate, and requests are only allowed if there are tokens available in the bucket. Once a request is processed, a token is removed from the bucket. If the bucket is empty, requests are blocked until more tokens become available.

Sliding window algorithm: Another approach is to use a sliding window algorithm, where a fixed number of requests are allowed within a specified time window. Requests that exceed this limit are blocked until the window resets. This approach can be more flexible than the token bucket algorithm, as it allows for bursts of requests within a specified time period.

Exponential backoff: Exponential backoff is a technique where the system gradually increases the delay between requests if a certain threshold is exceeded. For example, if a client exceeds the rate limit, the system can increase the time between requests exponentially until the rate limit is no longer exceeded.

Distributed rate limiting: In a distributed system, it may be necessary to implement rate limiting across multiple nodes. This can be achieved using techniques such as a centralized rate limiting service or distributed rate limiting using a consensus algorithm.

Example:

Consider an e-commerce website that needs to limit the number of requests a user can make to the API in order to prevent abuse and ensure fair usage. To implement rate limiting, the system could use a token bucket algorithm, where a fixed number of tokens are generated at a set rate, and requests are only allowed if there are tokens available in the bucket. Once a request is processed, a token is removed from the bucket. If the bucket is empty, requests are blocked until more tokens become available.

Alternatively, the system could use a sliding window algorithm, where a fixed number of requests are allowed within a specified time window. Requests that exceed this limit are blocked until the window resets. This approach can be more flexible than the token bucket algorithm, as it allows for bursts of requests within a specified time period.

In a distributed system, it may be necessary to implement rate limiting across multiple nodes. This can be achieved using techniques such as a centralized rate limiting service or distributed rate limiting using a consensus algorithm. A centralized rate limiting service could use a token bucket or sliding window algorithm to manage the rate limit across all nodes in the system. Alternatively, a distributed consensus algorithm such as Paxos or Raft could be used to ensure that all nodes in the system are enforcing the same rate limit.

4.4 Can you discuss the importance of versioning in APIs, and what are some best practices for managing API versions?

Versioning is an important aspect of API design, as it allows for the evolution of an API while maintaining backwards compatibility with existing clients. Here are some reasons why versioning is important in APIs:

Backwards compatibility: Versioning ensures that changes to an API do not break existing clients. By maintaining backwards compatibility, clients can continue to use the API without needing to modify their code.

Evolution: Versioning allows an API to evolve over time as requirements change. New features can be added, and existing features can be modified or deprecated without impacting existing clients.

Communication: Versioning allows for clear communication between API providers and consumers. It provides a mechanism for API providers to communicate changes to clients and for clients to understand the impact of those changes.

Best practices for managing API versions include:

Use semantic versioning: Semantic versioning is a widely used versioning scheme that provides a clear and consistent way to version APIs. Semantic versioning consists of three parts: major version, minor version, and patch version. Changes to the major version indicate backwards-incompatible changes, while changes to the minor and patch versions indicate backwards-compatible changes.

Use clear and descriptive version numbers: Version numbers should be clear and descriptive, so that clients can easily understand the significance of each version. For example, instead of using version numbers like "1.2" or "2.0", use version numbers like "v1.2.0" or "v2.0.0-beta".

Maintain backwards compatibility: When making changes to an API, strive to maintain backwards compatibility with existing clients. This can be achieved by using techniques like versioned endpoints, versioned headers, or content negotiation.

Provide clear documentation: When introducing new versions of an API, provide clear documentation that explains the differences between versions and how to upgrade from one version to another.

Sunset old versions: Eventually, old versions of an API should be sunsetted and deprecated. This ensures that clients are encouraged to upgrade to newer versions and that resources are not wasted maintaining deprecated versions.

Example:

Consider a social media platform that provides an API for third-party developers to access user data. The platform decides to make changes to the API to support new features, but wants to ensure that existing clients are not impacted by these changes. To manage API versions, the platform decides to use semantic versioning and introduces a new version of the API with the following changes:

Added support for private messages Modified the format of user profiles Deprecated the "likes" endpoint

The new version of the API is called "v2.0.0". The platform provides clear documentation that explains the differences between versions and how to upgrade from version "v1.0.0" to "v2.0.0". The platform also maintains backwards compatibility by using versioned endpoints and versioned headers. Finally, the platform decides to sunset version "v1.0.0" after six months to encourage clients to upgrade to the new version.

4.5   How do you approach designing a system for handling time-series data?

Designing a system for handling time-series data requires careful consideration of factors such as data volume, data frequency, data retention, data querying and analytics, and system performance. Here are some key considerations when designing such a system:

Data volume: Time-series data tends to accumulate quickly, so the system must be designed to handle large volumes of data. This requires careful consideration of storage requirements, data compression, and data partitioning strategies.

Data frequency: Time-series data is often generated at high frequency, such as sensor data or financial data. The system must be designed to handle high write throughput and provide efficient storage and retrieval of data.

Data retention: Time-series data can be valuable for historical analysis and trend analysis, so the system must be designed to retain data for extended periods of time. This requires careful consideration of storage capacity and retention policies.

Data querying and analytics: Time-series data is often used for analysis and visualization, so the system must support efficient querying and analytics. This requires careful consideration of indexing strategies, query performance, and data aggregation techniques.

System performance: The system must be designed to handle high read and write throughput, with minimal latency and downtime. This requires careful consideration of system architecture, load balancing strategies, and fault tolerance mechanisms.

Example:

Consider a system for handling time-series data from IoT devices in a manufacturing plant. The system must collect and store data from sensors across the plant, and provide real-time analytics and visualization for plant operators. To design such a system, we could follow these steps:

Determine data frequency and volume: The system must be designed to handle high-frequency data from sensors across the plant. We could estimate data volume by considering the number of sensors, the sampling rate, and the data size per sample.

Choose a data storage solution: For time-series data, a NoSQL database like Apache Cassandra or InfluxDB is often a good choice, as they provide efficient storage and retrieval of large volumes of data.

Choose a data retention policy: The system must be designed to retain data for extended periods of time for historical analysis. We could determine a retention policy by considering business requirements and storage capacity.

Design data models: The data model should be designed to efficiently store and retrieve time-series data. This could involve using partitioning strategies like time-based partitioning or geographic partitioning to optimize data access.

Optimize querying and analytics: The system must be designed to efficiently query and analyze time-series data. This could involve using indexing strategies to speed up queries, or using aggregation techniques to summarize data for visualization.

Design for performance: The system must be designed to handle high read and write throughput with minimal latency and downtime. This could involve using load balancing strategies like horizontal scaling, or implementing fault tolerance mechanisms like redundancy and failover.

By following these steps, we can design a system that efficiently handles time-series data and provides real-time analytics and visualization for plant operators.

4.6 How do you deal with eventual consistency and conflicts in a distributed system that uses optimistic concurrency control?

Optimistic concurrency control is a technique used to manage concurrency in distributed systems. It assumes that conflicts between concurrent operations are rare, and instead of blocking operations, it allows them to proceed and checks for conflicts only when updating the data. However, this approach can lead to eventual consistency issues if two or more operations conflict with each other. Here are some strategies to deal with eventual consistency and conflicts in a distributed system that uses optimistic concurrency control:

Conflict detection: The system should be designed to detect conflicts as soon as they occur. This could involve using timestamps or version numbers to track changes to the data, and comparing them when updating the data.

Conflict resolution: Once conflicts are detected, the system should be designed to resolve them in a consistent manner. This could involve using a conflict resolution algorithm that determines which operation takes precedence, or merging conflicting changes to the data.

Retry logic: If conflicts are detected, the system could retry the operation after a short delay, to allow time for other concurrent operations to complete. This could involve using an exponential backoff algorithm to progressively increase the delay between retries.

Compensation logic: If conflicts cannot be resolved, the system could use compensation logic to undo the effects of conflicting operations. This could involve rolling back the changes made by the conflicting operation and notifying the user of the conflict.

Example:

Consider a distributed system that allows multiple users to update a shared document. The system uses optimistic concurrency control to manage concurrency, but conflicts can occur if two or more users try to update the same portion of the document simultaneously. To deal with eventual consistency and conflicts, we could follow these steps:

Conflict detection: The system should track changes to the document using timestamps or version numbers, and compare them when updating the document. If conflicts are detected, the system should notify the user and prompt them to resolve the conflict.

Conflict resolution: If conflicts occur, the system should use a conflict resolution algorithm to determine which operation takes precedence. For example, the algorithm could give priority to the operation with the most recent timestamp or version number.

Retry logic: If conflicts are detected, the system could retry the operation after a short delay. The delay could be progressively increased using an exponential backoff algorithm, to avoid overwhelming the system with retries.

Compensation logic: If conflicts cannot be resolved, the system could use compensation logic to undo the effects of conflicting operations. For example, if two users try to delete the same portion of the document, the system could roll back the deletion and notify the users of the conflict.

By following these steps, we can design a system that uses optimistic concurrency control to manage concurrency and deals with eventual consistency and conflicts in a consistent and reliable manner.

4.7 Can you discuss different consistency models in distributed systems, such as strong consistency, weak consistency, and causal consistency?

In distributed systems, consistency refers to the degree to which all nodes in the system agree on the state of shared data. Different consistency models exist, each with its tradeoffs in terms of availability, performance, and fault tolerance. Some common consistency models are:

Strong consistency: In a strongly consistent system, all nodes see the same view of the data at all times. This consistency model requires all updates to be applied synchronously and ensures that read operations always return the latest committed value. However, strong consistency can lead to higher latency and reduced availability due to the need for synchronous updates.

Weak consistency: In a weakly consistent system, nodes can have different views of the data at any given time. This consistency model allows for eventual consistency, where updates propagate to all nodes over time, but it does not guarantee that read operations always return the latest committed value. Weak consistency is more scalable and available than strong consistency, but it can lead to inconsistencies and conflicts between different views of the data.

Eventual consistency: In an eventually consistent system, nodes eventually converge to the same view of the data over time, but there may

be periods where different nodes have different views of the data.
This consistency model is appropriate for systems where strong consistency is not required, and the system can tolerate temporary inconsistencies. Eventual consistency can achieve high availability and
scalability, but it requires careful design to manage conflicts and inconsistencies.

Causal consistency: In a causally consistent system, nodes can have
different views of the data, but the order of causally related operations
is preserved. This consistency model ensures that operations that
causally depend on each other are ordered correctly, but it allows for
temporary inconsistencies between other operations.

Example:

Consider a distributed system that allows multiple users to update a
shared document. The system can use different consistency models
to manage concurrency and ensure consistency. For example:

Strong consistency: In a strongly consistent system, all users see the
same view of the document at all times. When a user updates the
document, the update is applied synchronously to all replicas, ensuring that all users see the latest version of the document. However,
this approach can lead to high latency and reduced availability if the
system is under heavy load.

Weak consistency: In a weakly consistent system, users can have different views of the document at any given time. When a user updates
the document, the update is applied asynchronously to all replicas,
and users may see different versions of the document until updates
propagate to all replicas. This approach allows for greater scalability
and availability, but it can lead to temporary inconsistencies between
different views of the document.

Eventual consistency: In an eventually consistent system, users can
have different views of the document, but updates eventually propagate to all replicas, ensuring that all users eventually see the same
version of the document. This approach allows for high scalability
and availability, but it requires careful design to manage conflicts
and inconsistencies.

Causal consistency: In a causally consistent system, updates to the
document are ordered according to their causal dependencies. For

example, if one user adds a comment to a document, and another user replies to the comment, the reply is ordered after the comment. This approach ensures that causally related updates are ordered correctly, but it allows for temporary inconsistencies between other updates.

By choosing the appropriate consistency model, we can design a system that balances the tradeoffs between consistency, availability, and scalability based on the requirements of the application.

4.8 What are some strategies for implementing efficient search functionality in a large-scale system?

Efficient search functionality is critical for many large-scale systems, such as e-commerce platforms, social media networks, and search engines. Here are some strategies for implementing efficient search functionality in a large-scale system:

Use an indexing system: Indexing systems such as Elasticsearch, Solr, and Apache Lucene can improve search performance by preprocessing and indexing data for fast retrieval. These systems support complex queries, filtering, sorting, and faceting, and they can handle large volumes of data efficiently.

Use caching: Caching can reduce search latency by storing frequently accessed data in memory. By caching search results, we can avoid re-executing expensive queries and reduce the load on the underlying data store. Caching can be implemented using in-memory caches such as Redis or Memcached.

Use sharding: Sharding involves partitioning data across multiple nodes to improve scalability and performance. By distributing search requests across multiple shards, we can reduce the load on individual nodes and improve search throughput. Sharding can be implemented using tools such as Apache Cassandra, MongoDB, or MySQL.

Use denormalization: Denormalization involves duplicating data across multiple tables or collections to reduce the need for expensive joins and improve search performance. By storing frequently accessed data in a denormalized form, we can reduce the number of queries required to retrieve data and improve search latency.

Use machine learning: Machine learning techniques such as natural language processing and deep learning can improve search relevance and accuracy by understanding user intent and context. By analyzing user behavior and feedback, we can train models to deliver more relevant search results and improve the overall user experience.

Use query optimization: Query optimization involves analyzing search queries and optimizing them for faster execution. Techniques such as query rewriting, query planning, and query execution optimization can improve search performance and reduce query latency.

Example:

Suppose we are designing a large-scale e-commerce platform that supports search functionality. To implement efficient search, we could use the following strategies:

Use Elasticsearch for indexing and searching products: Elasticsearch can index product data in real-time and support complex search queries, filtering, and sorting. By using Elasticsearch, we can improve search performance and accuracy and handle large volumes of data efficiently.

Use Redis for caching frequently accessed search results: Redis can cache search results in memory, reducing the need to re-execute expensive queries and improving search latency. By caching frequently accessed search results, we can reduce the load on Elasticsearch and improve overall system performance.

Use sharding to partition product data across multiple nodes: By sharding product data across multiple nodes, we can distribute search requests and reduce the load on individual nodes. This can improve search throughput and handle increased traffic and load.

Use denormalization to store frequently accessed data in a denormalized form: By denormalizing product data, we can reduce the need for expensive joins and improve search performance. For example, we could store product descriptions, specifications, and reviews in a denormalized form to reduce the number of queries required to retrieve data.

By combining these strategies, we can design a system that delivers fast, accurate, and relevant search results for our users.

4.9 How do you design a system that can handle real-time data processing and analytics?

Designing a system that can handle real-time data processing and analytics requires careful consideration of several factors, including data volume, data velocity, data variety, and data complexity. Here are some key steps involved in designing a system that can handle real-time data processing and analytics:

Define the problem and use case: The first step is to clearly define the problem we are trying to solve and the use case for real-time data processing and analytics. For example, we may want to monitor website traffic in real-time, detect anomalies, and trigger alerts when traffic exceeds certain thresholds.

Identify the data sources and ingestion method: The next step is to identify the data sources and the method for ingesting data into the system. This may involve using tools such as Apache Kafka, Amazon Kinesis, or Apache Flume to stream data in real-time from sources such as web servers, IoT devices, or social media platforms.

Choose a data processing framework: There are several data processing frameworks available for real-time data processing and analytics, including Apache Storm, Apache Flink, and Apache Spark Streaming. These frameworks can process data streams in real-time, perform analytics, and generate insights.

Design the data storage and retrieval layer: Depending on the use case, we may need to store data in a relational or non-relational database, such as Apache Cassandra, MongoDB, or Elasticsearch. We may also need to design a retrieval layer that allows users to query and retrieve data in real-time.

Implement data visualization and reporting: To make sense of the data and insights generated by the system, we may need to implement data visualization and reporting tools such as Kibana, Tableau, or Power BI. These tools can help users understand the data and make informed decisions based on the insights generated by the system.

Example:

Suppose we are designing a real-time data processing and analytics system for a social media platform. The system needs to monitor user activity in real-time, perform sentiment analysis, and generate insights for the marketing team. Here are the steps we could follow to design the system:

Define the problem and use case: The problem we are trying to solve is to monitor user activity in real-time, detect sentiment, and generate insights for the marketing team to improve engagement.

Identify the data sources and ingestion method: The data sources include social media platforms such as Twitter and Facebook. We can use Apache Kafka to stream data in real-time from these sources.

Choose a data processing framework: We can use Apache Spark Streaming to process the data streams in real-time, perform sentiment analysis using natural language processing techniques, and generate insights.

Design the data storage and retrieval layer: We can store the data in a NoSQL database such as MongoDB or Cassandra, which can handle large volumes of data and provide fast retrieval. We can also design a retrieval layer that allows users to query and retrieve data in real-time.

Implement data visualization and reporting: We can use Kibana or Tableau to visualize the data and generate reports for the marketing team. These tools can help the team understand the insights generated by the system and make informed decisions to improve engagement.

By following these steps, we can design a real-time data processing and analytics system that can handle large volumes of data, perform analytics in real-time, and generate insights for the marketing team.

4.10 Can you explain the concept of quorum in the context of distributed systems, and why it's important?

In distributed systems, quorum refers to the minimum number of nodes that need to be available and responsive for the system to function properly. Quorum is important because it ensures that the system can still operate even if some nodes are unavailable or have failed.

A quorum can be defined as a simple majority of nodes, or it can be a more complex formula based on the total number of nodes in the system. For example, in a system with 5 nodes, a quorum might be defined as 3, meaning that at least 3 nodes must be available and responsive for the system to function properly.

Quorum is particularly important for systems that use distributed consensus algorithms, such as the Paxos or Raft algorithms, to ensure data consistency and prevent conflicts. These algorithms rely on a majority of nodes agreeing on a decision or a value, and without a quorum, the system can become fragmented and inconsistent.

For example, let's say we have a distributed database system that uses the Paxos algorithm for consensus. The system consists of 5 nodes, and a quorum is defined as 3. If 2 nodes fail, the system can still function because there are still 3 nodes available, which is the required quorum. However, if more than 2 nodes fail, the system will no longer be able to function because there are not enough nodes available to achieve the required quorum.

In summary, quorum is a critical concept in distributed systems that helps ensure system availability and consistency, particularly in systems that rely on distributed consensus algorithms.

4.11   How do you ensure data security and privacy in a distributed system?

Ensuring data security and privacy in a distributed system is critical to protecting sensitive information and preventing unauthorized access or data breaches. Here are some strategies that can be used to achieve this:

Encryption: Data encryption is a common strategy used to protect data from unauthorized access. Encryption can be applied at various levels, including transport encryption, which secures data in transit between nodes, and storage encryption, which secures data at rest. Encryption keys can also be managed centrally to ensure consistent security across the distributed system.

Access control: Access control mechanisms can be implemented to restrict access to sensitive data to authorized users or applications. This can include authentication and authorization protocols, such as OAuth, OpenID Connect, or LDAP, that allow users to access data only if they have the appropriate permissions.

Auditing and monitoring: Regular auditing and monitoring of system activity can help identify and prevent potential security threats. This can include logging system activity, analyzing system logs to identify suspicious activity, and using intrusion detection systems to alert administrators of potential security breaches.

Redundancy and failover: Ensuring redundancy and failover capabilities in a distributed system can help prevent data loss or corruption in the event of a security breach or other system failure. This can include replicating data across multiple nodes, using backup and recovery mechanisms, and implementing disaster recovery plans.

Compliance and regulation: Compliance with relevant regulations and standards, such as HIPAA or PCI DSS, can help ensure that the system meets established security requirements and guidelines. This can include regular security assessments, vulnerability scanning, and penetration testing.

For example, let's say we have a distributed healthcare system that stores sensitive patient data. To ensure data security and privacy, the system could implement encryption at the transport and storage level, use access control mechanisms to restrict access to sensitive data, regularly audit and monitor system activity, and ensure redundancy and failover capabilities in the event of a security breach or system failure. The system could also comply with relevant regulations and standards, such as HIPAA, to ensure that it meets established security requirements and guidelines.

In summary, ensuring data security and privacy in a distributed system requires a multi-layered approach that includes encryption, access control, auditing and monitoring, redundancy and failover, and compliance with relevant regulations and standards.

4.12 What is the role of a consensus algorithm in a distributed system, and can you discuss some common examples?

In a distributed system, a consensus algorithm is used to ensure that all nodes in the system agree on the same state, even in the presence of failures or network partitions. The goal of a consensus algorithm is to ensure that the system remains available and consistent, even in the face of failures or network disruptions.

Consensus algorithms work by allowing nodes in the system to communicate with each other and agree on a shared state. This shared state can represent a variety of things, such as the current value of a distributed database or the leader node in a distributed cluster.

One common example of a consensus algorithm is the Paxos algorithm. The Paxos algorithm is used to ensure that nodes in a distributed system agree on a shared value, even in the presence of failures. The algorithm works by allowing nodes to communicate with each other and propose a value. Nodes then vote on the proposed value, and if a majority of nodes agree on the value, it becomes the new shared value. The Paxos algorithm is widely used in distributed systems such as Apache ZooKeeper and Google Chubby.

Another common example of a consensus algorithm is the Raft algorithm. The Raft algorithm is used to ensure that a group of nodes in a distributed system agree on a shared leader node. The algorithm works by electing a leader node, which is responsible for coordinating operations within the system. If the leader node fails or becomes unavailable, a new leader node is elected to take its place. The Raft algorithm is widely used in distributed systems such as etcd and CockroachDB.

In summary, consensus algorithms play a critical role in ensuring that distributed systems remain available and consistent, even in the presence of failures or network disruptions. Some common examples of consensus algorithms include the Paxos algorithm and the Raft algorithm, both of which are widely used in distributed systems today.

4.13 Can you discuss strategies for implementing graceful degradation in a system?

Graceful degradation is a strategy used in system design to ensure that a system remains available and functional, even in the face of failures or network disruptions. The goal of graceful degradation is to provide a degraded but still usable service to users, rather than a complete outage.

There are several strategies that can be used to implement graceful degradation in a system, including:

Load shedding: Load shedding is a strategy used to manage system overload by shedding non-critical requests. This can be accomplished by prioritizing requests based on their importance, and dropping requests that exceed the system's capacity.

Circuit breaking: Circuit breaking is a strategy used to detect failures and prevent them from propagating throughout the system. This can be accomplished by implementing a circuit breaker pattern that monitors system health and isolates failing components.

Fallbacks: Fallbacks are alternative strategies or services that can be used when the primary service is unavailable. This can be accomplished by implementing a fallback mechanism that redirects requests to a secondary service or data source.

Timeouts: Timeouts are a strategy used to prevent system overload by limiting the amount of time a request can take to complete. This can be accomplished by implementing a timeout mechanism that cancels requests that exceed a certain time threshold.

Graceful degradation modes: Graceful degradation modes are predefined states in a system that are triggered in response to failures or network disruptions. These modes can be used to provide a degraded but still usable service to users, rather than a complete outage.

For example, consider a web application that allows users to search for products. If the search service becomes overloaded, the application could implement a fallback mechanism that redirects searches to a secondary search service or database. Additionally, the application could implement a circuit breaker pattern that detects failures and isolates failing components to prevent them from impacting the entire system.

In summary, implementing graceful degradation in a system is an important strategy for ensuring that the system remains available and functional, even in the face of failures or network disruptions. Strategies such as load shedding, circuit breaking, fallbacks, timeouts, and graceful degradation modes can all be used to implement graceful degradation in a system.

4.14   How do you design an efficient notification system that can handle a large number of users?

Designing an efficient notification system that can handle a large number of users requires careful consideration of various factors such as scalability, reliability, security, and performance. Here are some key steps that can be followed to design such a system:

Choose the right messaging platform: Choosing the right messaging platform is critical to building a scalable and reliable notification system. Some popular messaging platforms include Apache Kafka, RabbitMQ, and Amazon Simple Notification Service (SNS). These platforms offer features such as pub/sub messaging, scalability, high availability, and fault tolerance.

Use a distributed system architecture: To handle a large number of users, it is important to use a distributed system architecture that can scale horizontally. The architecture should also be designed to handle failures gracefully and provide high availability.

Implement message queues: To manage the delivery of notifications, it is important to implement message queues. Message queues can help to reduce the load on the notification server and ensure that messages are delivered reliably and efficiently.

Use push notifications: Push notifications are a popular way of delivering notifications to mobile devices. They can be implemented using platforms such as Apple Push Notification Service (APNS) and Google Cloud Messaging (GCM). Push notifications help to reduce the load on the server by allowing devices to receive notifications directly.

Optimize message delivery: To ensure that notifications are delivered efficiently, it is important to optimize the message delivery process. This can be accomplished by using techniques such as message batching, message compression, and message routing.

Ensure security and privacy: Notifications often contain sensitive information, so it is important to ensure that the notification system is secure and privacy-compliant. This can be accomplished by implementing encryption, access controls, and authentication mechanisms.

Monitor and optimize performance: It is important to monitor the performance of the notification system and optimize it to ensure that it meets the performance requirements. This can be accomplished by monitoring metrics such as message delivery rate, latency, and error rates, and optimizing the system accordingly.

For example, consider a social media application that needs to send notifications to a large number of users. The application could use a messaging platform such as Apache Kafka to handle message delivery and implement message queues to manage the delivery of notifications. Push notifications could be used to deliver notifications to mobile devices, and the system could be designed to scale horizontally to handle increasing numbers of users.

In summary, designing an efficient notification system that can handle a large number of users requires careful consideration of various factors such as scalability, reliability, security, and performance. By following the key steps outlined above, it is possible to design a notification system that can deliver notifications reliably and efficiently to a large number of users.

4.15   What are some challenges associated with designing systems that need to handle geographically distributed data?

Designing systems that need to handle geographically distributed data comes with several challenges, including:

Latency: When data is distributed across multiple locations, it takes more time to access it due to the longer physical distance involved. This increased latency can cause performance issues, especially for applications that require real-time or near-real-time access to the data.

Data consistency: Maintaining data consistency across different locations is another challenge. In a distributed system, different nodes may have different versions of the same data, and ensuring that these versions are synchronized can be complex.

Network connectivity: Network connectivity is crucial when working with geographically distributed data. System designers need to consider factors such as bandwidth, reliability, and security to ensure that data can be transferred between locations efficiently and securely.

Data privacy and compliance: Different regions may have different data privacy laws and regulations, and it can be challenging to ensure compliance across all locations. This is particularly important for sensitive data such as personally identifiable information (PII).

Data partitioning: Designing a distributed system that can handle geographically distributed data often requires partitioning data across multiple locations. This can be complex, especially when dealing with large datasets or when the data needs to be distributed in a way that supports specific access patterns.

To address these challenges, system designers may use a range of techniques and technologies, such as:

Data replication: Replicating data across multiple locations can help improve data availability and reduce latency. However, this approach can also increase complexity and make it harder to maintain data consistency.

Content delivery networks (CDNs): CDNs can be used to distribute content across multiple locations, reducing latency and improving performance for end-users.

Caching: Caching frequently accessed data can help reduce latency and improve performance.

Network optimization: Optimizing network connectivity between different locations can help improve performance and reduce latency.

Data partitioning: Partitioning data in a way that supports specific access patterns can help improve performance and scalability.

Compliance frameworks: Implementing compliance frameworks can help ensure that data is handled in compliance with relevant laws and regulations.

4.16 Can you discuss the trade-offs between push and pull models in data processing and communication?

Push and pull models are two different approaches for data processing and communication in a system. In a push model, data is actively sent to the receiver without waiting for a request or query from the receiver. In contrast, in a pull model, the receiver sends a request or query to the sender, which then sends the data in response.

Both models have their own advantages and disadvantages, and the choice between them largely depends on the specific requirements and constraints of the system being designed.

Push models are generally better suited for real-time systems that require quick and immediate processing of data. For example, a system that monitors the performance of a stock market may use a push model to send real-time data updates to traders and analysts, so that they can react quickly to changes in the market. Another example is a social media platform that sends push notifications to users when someone likes or comments on their posts.

Push models are also beneficial when the sender has a large amount of data to send and the receiver needs to be continuously updated with the latest information. For instance, a weather monitoring system may use a push model to send updates on weather patterns to subscribers in a particular region.

However, push models can also result in high network traffic and may overload the receiver with data that is not immediately needed, resulting in inefficiencies. Additionally, if the receiver is offline or experiences connectivity issues, the push model may result in data loss.

On the other hand, pull models are generally better suited for systems where data is not needed in real-time and the receiver can wait for data to be delivered as requested. This can result in more efficient use of network resources, as data is only sent when it is needed. An example of a pull model is a web browser that sends a request for a webpage and receives the response containing the page's content.

Pull models can also be beneficial when the receiver has limited processing power or storage capacity, as it can selectively request only the data that is needed. Additionally, pull models can provide a level of control over the data being received, as the receiver can specify exactly what data is needed.

However, pull models may not be suitable for systems that require real-time updates or where the receiver needs to be continuously updated with the latest data. Additionally, pull models may result in latency issues if the receiver needs to wait for data to be delivered.

In conclusion, the choice between push and pull models largely depends on the specific requirements and constraints of the system being designed. It is important to carefully consider the trade-offs between the two models and choose the approach that best meets the needs of the system.

4.17   How do you design a system for efficiently handling large file uploads and downloads?

Designing a system that can efficiently handle large file uploads and downloads is a common requirement for many applications. Here are some strategies that can be used to achieve this:

Use chunking: Chunking involves splitting large files into smaller pieces, which can then be uploaded or downloaded independently. This approach can help to avoid network interruptions or timeouts that can occur when transferring large files all at once. It also allows for parallel processing of each chunk, which can speed up the overall transfer process.

Compression: Compressing files before transfer can help to reduce the size of the data being transferred, which can make the transfer process faster and more efficient. This is particularly useful for large files that contain many repeated patterns or text.

Use Content Delivery Networks (CDNs): CDNs are geographically distributed networks of servers that can cache and serve content to users from the closest available server. This can help to reduce the distance that data needs to travel and can therefore speed up file transfers.

Use parallelism: Parallelism involves breaking up a task into smaller pieces that can be processed simultaneously. For example, multiple files can be uploaded or downloaded at the same time, or different parts of a large file can be transferred in parallel.

Use resumable transfers: Resumable transfers allow for uploads or downloads to be resumed from the point of failure, rather than having to start the entire process over again. This can be particularly useful for large files that may take a long time to upload or download.

Use dedicated file transfer protocols: There are many protocols designed specifically for large file transfers, such as File Transfer Protocol (FTP) or Secure Copy (SCP). These protocols can provide faster and more reliable transfers than standard HTTP-based transfers.

By implementing these strategies, a system can be designed to efficiently handle large file uploads and downloads. However, it is important to keep in mind that each approach has its own trade-offs and limitations, and the optimal approach will depend on the specific needs of the system and the users.

4.18 What are some strategies for handling hotspots in distributed systems, such as hot partitions or hot keys?

In distributed systems, hotspots refer to the parts of the system that receive a disproportionate amount of traffic or requests compared to other parts of the system. Hotspots can occur due to various reasons, such as skewed data distribution, popular items, or frequently accessed data. Hotspots can lead to degraded performance, increased response times, and even system failures.

To handle hotspots in distributed systems, several strategies can be employed:

Data partitioning: Partitioning the data can help distribute the load across multiple nodes, and avoid hotspots by evenly distributing the data. There are different partitioning strategies such as key-based partitioning, range-based partitioning, and hash-based partitioning.

Caching: Caching frequently accessed data can help reduce the load on the system, especially for read-heavy workloads. Popular caching technologies include Redis, Memcached, and Hazelcast.

Load balancing: Load balancing helps distribute the incoming requests across multiple nodes, ensuring that no single node becomes a hotspot. Load balancers can be implemented using software or hardware, and they can balance the load based on different criteria such as round-robin, IP hashing, or least connections.

Replication: Replicating the data across multiple nodes can help improve read performance and reduce the load on individual nodes. There are different replication strategies such as master-slave, master-master, and multi-master.

Data denormalization: In some cases, denormalizing the data can help avoid hotspots by reducing the number of joins required for a query. Denormalization involves duplicating data across multiple tables or columns, which can help speed up queries and reduce the load on individual nodes.

Application-level sharding: Sharding at the application level involves partitioning the data based on application-level criteria, such as user IDs, geolocation, or product categories. This approach can help avoid hotspots by ensuring that the data is evenly distributed across multiple nodes.

It's important to note that each strategy has its own trade-offs in terms of complexity, consistency, and scalability. The appropriate strategy depends on the specific requirements of the system and the trade-offs that are acceptable for the application.

4.19   Can you discuss techniques for optimizing system performance through caching, such as cache eviction policies and cache hierarchy?

Caching is a commonly used technique in system design for improving performance by storing frequently accessed data in a faster, closer location to the user or application. Here are some techniques for optimizing system performance through caching:

Cache eviction policies: When the cache reaches its maximum size, some data must be removed to make room for new data. The way in which data is selected for removal is known as the cache eviction policy. There are several popular cache eviction policies, such as Least Recently Used (LRU), First In First Out (FIFO), and Random Replacement.

Cache hierarchy: In large-scale systems, it's common to have multiple levels of caching to provide optimal performance. The highest level of cache, often referred to as the first-level cache, is typically a small, fast cache that's located closest to the application or user. As the cache size increases, the lower levels of the cache can be optimized for larger data sets.

Cache partitioning: In distributed systems, caching can be used to improve performance by reducing the load on the network and the backend servers. One technique for caching in distributed systems is cache partitioning, where the cache is divided into multiple partitions, each responsible for a specific subset of the data. This allows for more efficient caching and reduces the risk of hotspots in the cache.

Content Delivery Networks (CDNs): A CDN is a globally distributed network of servers that are used to deliver content to users from the server that is closest to them. By caching content on servers around the world, CDNs can greatly reduce the latency and improve the performance of applications that rely on delivering large amounts of content, such as video streaming or social media.

In-memory databases: In-memory databases can also be used to improve performance by caching data in memory instead of on disk. This can provide a significant performance boost, especially for read-heavy workloads, but can be limited by the amount of available memory.

Overall, caching is an important technique for optimizing system performance and reducing the load on backend servers. By choosing the right caching strategy and implementing it effectively, system designers can greatly improve the user experience and the overall performance of the system.

4.20   How do you handle data retention and archiving in a system that generates a large volume of data over time?

Data retention and archiving are essential aspects of system design, especially for systems that generate a large volume of data over time. The goal of data retention is to ensure that the system has access to historical data, while the goal of data archiving is to preserve data for long-term storage and compliance purposes.

When designing a system for data retention and archiving, some key considerations include the types of data being generated, the volume of data, the desired retention period, and any compliance or regulatory requirements. Some strategies for handling data retention and archiving in a system include:

Partitioning data: One approach is to partition data into separate databases or storage systems based on age or other criteria. This allows for more efficient management of data and faster access to more recent data.

Tying retention to business requirements: Retention policies should be tied to business requirements to ensure that data is retained only for as long as it is needed. This helps to minimize storage costs and reduce the risk of non-compliance with regulations.

Implementing a tiered storage architecture: A tiered storage architecture involves storing data on multiple types of storage media based on factors such as access frequency, data type, and age. This helps to optimize storage costs while still ensuring that data is available when needed.

Using compression and deduplication: Compression and deduplication techniques can be used to reduce the amount of storage space required for data retention and archiving.

Implementing backup and recovery procedures: Backup and recovery procedures are essential for ensuring that data is not lost due to hardware failure, natural disasters, or other catastrophic events.

Utilizing cloud storage solutions: Cloud storage solutions offer cost-effective and scalable options for data retention and archiving. Cloud-based solutions can also provide added redundancy and disaster recovery capabilities.

In summary, designing a system for efficient data retention and archiving involves careful consideration of the types of data being generated, the desired retention period, compliance and regulatory requirements, and other factors. By implementing strategies such as partitioning data, tiered storage, compression and deduplication, backup and recovery procedures, and cloud storage solutions, a system can efficiently handle large volumes of data over time.

Chapter 5

Expert

5.1 Can you discuss the challenges and best practices in designing a globally distributed, multi-region system?

Designing a globally distributed, multi-region system poses a unique set of challenges that need to be addressed to ensure the system's success. Here are some of the key challenges and best practices to keep in mind:

Challenges Latency: With data centers spread across multiple regions, users may experience latency issues, which can affect the system's performance and user experience. Data consistency: Maintaining data consistency across multiple regions can be challenging due to the potential for conflicts and delays in data propagation. Network reliability: A distributed system relies heavily on the network to transfer data between regions. Network failures or disruptions can result in data loss or system downtime. Regulatory compliance: Different regions may have different laws and regulations that must be adhered to, which can impact the design and implementation of the system. Cost and complexity: Building and managing a globally distributed system can be expensive and complex, requiring significant resources and expertise. Best practices Geographic load balanc-

ing: Use a global traffic management solution that can route users to
the closest data center, reducing latency and improving performance.
Data replication and synchronization: Replicate data across multiple
regions and implement a synchronization mechanism to ensure data
consistency. Resiliency and redundancy: Ensure the system is resilient to network failures by implementing redundancy and failover
mechanisms. Compliance and security: Ensure the system complies
with regulatory requirements and follows best practices for security,
such as encrypting data in transit and at rest. Monitoring and testing: Implement a robust monitoring and testing strategy to detect
and resolve issues before they impact users.

For example, a global e-commerce platform may have data centers in
North America, Europe, and Asia. To ensure the system is optimized
for performance and reliability, the platform may use a global traffic
management solution to route users to the closest data center. To
maintain data consistency, the platform may replicate data across all
data centers and use a synchronization mechanism to ensure updates
are propagated in a timely manner. To ensure resiliency and redundancy, the platform may use load balancing and failover mechanisms
to handle network failures and ensure the system is always available.
Finally, the platform may implement strict security measures to protect user data and comply with relevant regulations, such as GDPR
in Europe.

5.2 How do you approach designing a sys-tem with support for multi-tenancy and data isolation?

Multi-tenancy is an architectural approach where a single software
application serves multiple clients, called tenants, each with its own
isolated data and configuration. A multi-tenant system must ensure
that data belonging to one tenant is not accessible or visible to another tenant.

Designing a system with multi-tenancy and data isolation involves
the following steps:

Tenant Identification: The system must have a way to identify the tenant for whom the data belongs. This can be achieved through several methods, such as subdomains, unique IDs, or user accounts. Each tenant should have its own unique identifier, which can be used to isolate their data.

Data Isolation: Once the tenant is identified, the system should ensure that the data of one tenant is isolated from other tenants. This can be achieved through several methods, such as separate databases, schemas, tables, or rows. Each tenant's data should be logically separated to prevent unauthorized access to sensitive information.

Tenant Configuration: The system must allow each tenant to configure its own settings, such as branding, customization, and access control. This can be achieved through configurable settings, such as configuration files, database tables, or application settings.

Tenant Provisioning: The system must provide a mechanism to onboard new tenants and provision their data and configuration. This can be achieved through a self-service portal, API, or manual provisioning process.

Scalability: A multi-tenant system must be scalable to handle a large number of tenants and their data. This can be achieved through horizontal scaling by adding more resources, such as servers, storage, or databases.

Security: A multi-tenant system must ensure that the data of each tenant is secured and protected from unauthorized access or malicious attacks. This can be achieved through several methods, such as encryption, access control, and monitoring.

Performance: A multi-tenant system must ensure that the performance of the system is not impacted by the presence of multiple tenants. This can be achieved through several methods, such as caching, load balancing, and database partitioning.

Overall, designing a system with multi-tenancy and data isolation requires careful consideration of the unique needs of each tenant and their data, as well as the performance and scalability requirements of the system.

5.3   What are some strategies for handling data deduplication and compression in large-scale systems?

Data deduplication and compression are important techniques used to optimize storage and bandwidth utilization in large-scale systems.

Data deduplication is the process of identifying and eliminating redundant data within a system. This can be achieved by using techniques such as content-addressable storage, where data is stored based on its content rather than its location, and data hashing, where a unique hash is generated for each piece of data and used to identify duplicates. By eliminating redundant data, the amount of storage required can be significantly reduced, which can help to optimize system performance and reduce costs.

Compression is the process of reducing the size of data by encoding it in a more compact form. This can be achieved using various techniques, such as run-length encoding, where sequences of repeated values are replaced by a count and a single value, or Huffman encoding, where the most frequent values are assigned shorter codes than less frequent values. Compression can help to reduce the amount of data that needs to be transmitted or stored, which can improve system performance and reduce costs.

Some strategies for handling data deduplication and compression in large-scale systems include:

Using specialized hardware: Specialized hardware, such as storage arrays with built-in deduplication and compression capabilities, can help to offload the processing required for these tasks from the main system.

Using distributed systems: Distributed systems can be designed to handle data deduplication and compression in a more efficient manner. For example, data can be deduplicated and compressed at the source before it is transmitted to the central system, reducing the amount of data that needs to be transmitted.

Using hybrid storage systems: Hybrid storage systems can be used to combine the benefits of different storage technologies, such as solid-state drives (SSDs) and hard disk drives (HDDs), to optimize storage utilization. For example, frequently accessed data can be stored on SSDs, while less frequently accessed data can be stored on HDDs, and data can be compressed to reduce storage requirements.

Using data lifecycle management: Data lifecycle management can be used to automatically move data between different storage tiers based on its age or access patterns. This can help to ensure that data is stored in the most efficient manner possible, while still being readily accessible when needed.

In summary, data deduplication and compression are important techniques for optimizing storage and bandwidth utilization in large-scale systems. By using specialized hardware, distributed systems, hybrid storage systems, and data lifecycle management, these techniques can be applied in an efficient and effective manner.

5.4   How do you design a system with support for long-running transactions and distributed transactions?

Designing a system with support for long-running transactions and distributed transactions is a complex task that requires careful planning and consideration of several factors. Here are some strategies that can be used to design such a system:

Use a distributed transaction coordinator: A distributed transaction coordinator (DTC) is a component that manages distributed transactions across multiple databases or services. The DTC ensures that all parts of the transaction are committed or rolled back together, even if they are running on different machines. One example of a DTC is Microsoft's Distributed Transaction Coordinator (MSDTC).

Implement two-phase commit protocol: The two-phase commit (2PC) protocol is a standard protocol used to ensure that distributed transactions are atomic and consistent across multiple databases or services. In this protocol, the coordinator first asks all the participants to prepare for the commit by locking their resources. If all participants are ready, the coordinator then asks them to commit the transaction together. If any participant fails to commit, the coordinator rolls back the entire transaction.

Use compensating transactions: Compensating transactions are used to undo the effects of a transaction in case of a failure. If a distributed transaction fails, the compensating transaction is used to undo the changes made by the original transaction. This technique can be useful in situations where it is not possible to roll back a transaction using the 2PC protocol.

Implement timeout mechanisms: Long-running transactions can cause resource contention and lead to deadlocks. To avoid this, systems should implement timeout mechanisms that limit the duration of a transaction. If a transaction takes too long to complete, it should be rolled back automatically to free up resources.

Use optimistic concurrency control: Optimistic concurrency control (OCC) is a technique used to handle conflicts in distributed transactions. In this technique, each participant checks if its version of the data is still current before committing the transaction. If a participant detects a conflict, it rolls back the transaction and retries it.

Use event sourcing: Event sourcing is a technique used to store the state of a system as a sequence of events. This technique can be used to support long-running transactions by storing the events that represent the changes made by a transaction. If the transaction fails, the events can be discarded to roll back the changes.

In summary, designing a system with support for long-running transactions and distributed transactions requires careful consideration of factors such as data consistency, performance, and fault tolerance. By using techniques such as a distributed transaction coordinator, two-phase commit protocol, compensating transactions, timeout mechanisms, optimistic concurrency control, and event sourcing, it is possible to design a system that can handle such transactions efficiently and reliably.

5.5 Can you discuss the concept of a "shared nothing" architecture and its advantages and disadvantages?

The "shared nothing" architecture is a design approach for distributed systems where each node operates independently and does not share memory or disk storage with other nodes. Instead, each node has its own set of resources that it manages independently, and data is partitioned and distributed across the nodes in the system. This approach allows for high scalability, fault tolerance, and performance, as each node can operate independently without being affected by the failure or overload of other nodes.

Advantages of the shared nothing architecture include:

Scalability: The shared nothing architecture allows for easy horizontal scaling by simply adding more nodes to the system, without any need for shared memory or storage. This makes it easier to handle large amounts of data and high levels of traffic.

Fault tolerance: Because each node is independent, the failure of one node does not affect the rest of the system. This allows for high availability and fault tolerance, as the system can continue to operate even if one or more nodes fail.

Performance: By distributing data and processing across multiple nodes, the shared nothing architecture can achieve high performance and low latency, as each node can operate independently and in parallel.

Disadvantages of the shared nothing architecture include:

Complexity: Partitioning and distributing data across multiple nodes can be complex and require careful planning to ensure that data is evenly distributed and balanced across the system.

Data consistency: Because data is distributed across multiple nodes, maintaining data consistency can be challenging. This requires careful coordination and synchronization between nodes to ensure that all nodes have access to the same data.

Cost: Building and maintaining a shared nothing system can be expensive, as each node requires its own set of resources and management infrastructure.

Overall, the shared nothing architecture is a powerful design approach for building large-scale, distributed systems that require high scalability, fault tolerance, and performance. However, it requires careful planning and management to ensure that data is properly partitioned and distributed, and that data consistency is maintained across the system.

5.6 How do you ensure resilience and fault-tolerance in a system with many dependencies on external services?

Designing a system that is resilient and fault-tolerant can be challenging, especially when the system has many dependencies on external services. However, there are several strategies that can help ensure the system is resilient and can continue to function even when one or more dependencies fail.

One key strategy is to use redundancy and failover mechanisms. For example, instead of relying on a single external service, the system can use multiple redundant services that are configured to automatically fail over if one of them goes down. This can be achieved using load balancers or specialized software like service meshes that can automatically route traffic to healthy services.

Another strategy is to implement circuit breakers, which are mechanisms that can detect when an external service is experiencing problems and temporarily stop sending requests to that service. This can help prevent cascading failures that could bring down the entire system. Circuit breakers can be configured to automatically reset after a set amount of time, or they can be manually reset when the external service is back up and running.

In addition, designing systems with retry and timeout mechanisms can also help ensure resilience and fault-tolerance. If an external service is temporarily unavailable, the system can automatically retry the request after a set amount of time. If the request still fails after a certain number of retries, the system can time out and try an alternative service or take other action to prevent failure.

Finally, logging and monitoring can play a critical role in ensuring resilience and fault-tolerance in a system with many dependencies on external services. By monitoring the performance and availability of external services and logging any errors or failures, the system can quickly identify problems and take corrective action. This can help prevent failures from cascading through the system and minimize downtime.

Overall, ensuring resilience and fault-tolerance in a system with many dependencies on external services requires a combination of redundancy, failover mechanisms, circuit breakers, retry and timeout mechanisms, and robust logging and monitoring. By carefully designing and implementing these strategies, the system can continue to function even when individual dependencies fail.

5.7 Can you discuss strategies for implementing end-to-end encryption in a distributed system?

End-to-end encryption is a method of encrypting data at the source and decrypting it at the destination, thereby ensuring that the data remains confidential during transit. In a distributed system, end-to-end encryption is important to prevent unauthorized access to sensitive information, even if an attacker is able to compromise one or more nodes in the system. Here are some strategies for implementing end-to-end encryption in a distributed system:

Use public-key encryption: One common approach to end-to-end encryption is to use public-key encryption, such as RSA or ECC. With this approach, each user generates a public and private key pair. The user's public key is used to encrypt data, while the private key is used to decrypt it. When a user wants to send a message to another user, they encrypt the message using the recipient's public key. The recipient can then decrypt the message using their private key.

Implement perfect forward secrecy: Perfect forward secrecy (PFS) is a technique that generates a unique session key for each communication session. This means that even if an attacker is able to intercept and decrypt one session, they cannot use the same key to decrypt subsequent sessions. PFS can be implemented using techniques such as Diffie-Hellman key exchange.

Use symmetric encryption for data at rest: While public-key encryption is well-suited for securing data during transit, it can be slow and computationally expensive for encrypting data at rest. For this reason, it's often better to use symmetric encryption algorithms like AES for data at rest. In a distributed system, this can be implemented using a key management service that securely distributes keys to nodes that need to access the encrypted data.

Secure key management: A key management system is crucial for securely distributing and managing keys in a distributed system. Keys should be protected with strong encryption and access controls, and key rotation policies should be in place to ensure that compromised keys are quickly revoked.

Consider implementing homomorphic encryption: Homomorphic encryption is a type of encryption that allows computations to be performed on encrypted data without first decrypting it. This can be useful in distributed systems where sensitive data needs to be processed by multiple nodes without exposing the data to potential attackers.

Overall, implementing end-to-end encryption in a distributed system requires careful consideration of the unique security and performance requirements of the system.

5.8 How do you design a system to handle large-scale, real-time stream processing and complex event processing?

Designing a system to handle large-scale, real-time stream processing and complex event processing requires careful consideration of a number of factors. The system must be capable of handling large volumes of data in real time, detecting patterns and anomalies, and triggering appropriate actions based on the results of the analysis. Some strategies for designing such a system include:

Data ingestion: The system should be able to ingest data from multiple sources, such as sensors, log files, and social media feeds, in real time. It should be able to handle a large volume of data and be capable of handling different data formats.

Data processing: The system should be able to process the ingested data in real time and perform complex event processing to detect patterns and anomalies. This requires powerful analytics capabilities, including machine learning and artificial intelligence algorithms.

Data storage: The system should be able to store the processed data for later analysis and retrieval. The storage should be scalable and fault-tolerant, with built-in redundancy to ensure data availability.

Data visualization: The system should be able to present the processed data in a way that is easy to understand for users, such as dashboards or reports. The data should be presented in real time, allowing users to react to events as they happen.

Fault tolerance: The system should be designed to be fault-tolerant, with built-in redundancy and failover mechanisms to ensure the system can continue to function in the event of a hardware or software failure.

Scalability: The system should be designed to be scalable, allowing it to handle increasing volumes of data as the system grows. This requires careful consideration of the underlying architecture, including load balancing and distributed computing strategies.

Security: The system must be designed with security in mind, with appropriate encryption and access control measures to protect the data and prevent unauthorized access.

Examples of systems that require large-scale, real-time stream processing and complex event processing include financial trading systems, social media monitoring tools, and Internet of Things (IoT) applications. These systems require the ability to ingest large volumes of data in real time, process that data quickly and accurately, and trigger appropriate actions based on the results of the analysis. By following best practices in system design and architecture, it is possible to create a system that is capable of meeting these demanding requirements.

5.9   What are some strategies for designing a system with support for both online and offline processing?

In many systems, there is a need to support both online and offline processing. Online processing refers to real-time data processing that happens in response to user interactions or events. In contrast, offline processing refers to batch processing of data that is not time-sensitive and can be executed periodically.

Here are some strategies for designing a system with support for both online and offline processing:

Use stream processing: Stream processing is an approach to real-time data processing that allows you to process data as it arrives. Stream processing can be used to handle online processing requirements and can be combined with batch processing for offline processing. Apache Kafka and Apache Flink are examples of popular stream processing frameworks.

Utilize a message queue: A message queue can be used to buffer incoming data and provide a means of decoupling online and offline processing. Data can be ingested into the message queue in real-time, and then processed in batches later for offline processing. Apache Kafka and RabbitMQ are popular message queue solutions.

Implement a lambda architecture: A lambda architecture is an approach to designing a system that combines both batch and stream processing. The architecture consists of two layers: a batch layer and a speed layer. The batch layer is responsible for offline processing and the speed layer handles real-time processing. The results from both layers are combined to provide the final output. Apache Storm and Apache Spark are examples of popular lambda architecture frameworks.

Use cloud-based solutions: Many cloud providers offer services that support both online and offline processing, such as AWS Lambda, AWS Batch, and Google Cloud Dataflow. These services can be used to build scalable and fault-tolerant systems that can handle both types of processing.

Consider data partitioning: Data partitioning is a technique that involves dividing large datasets into smaller partitions. This can be useful for both online and offline processing, as it allows you to distribute processing across multiple machines and process data in parallel. Apache Cassandra and Apache Hadoop are examples of popular solutions that support data partitioning.

In summary, designing a system that can support both online and offline processing requires careful consideration of the processing requirements and data volumes. By using techniques such as stream processing, message queues, lambda architectures, cloud-based solutions, and data partitioning, you can build a system that can handle both types of processing efficiently and reliably.

5.10 How do you approach designing a system that requires complex data synchronization and conflict resolution?

Designing a system that requires complex data synchronization and conflict resolution can be a challenging task. The goal is to ensure that the data remains consistent and accurate across all nodes, even when multiple nodes are simultaneously updating the data.

Here are some strategies for designing such a system:

Conflict detection and resolution: The system should have a mechanism for detecting and resolving conflicts when they occur. This can involve timestamp-based conflict resolution or conflict resolution through voting.

Consistent data models: It is important to have consistent data models across all nodes. This can be achieved through schema versioning or by using a common data model.

Master-slave replication: In a master-slave replication model, the master node is responsible for all updates, while the slave nodes are read-only. This approach can simplify conflict resolution as it eliminates the possibility of conflicts occurring between multiple nodes making updates.

Two-phase commit: Two-phase commit is a protocol used to ensure that distributed transactions are either committed or aborted. It involves a coordinator node that initiates the transaction and communicates with all participating nodes to ensure that they are ready to commit the transaction. If any node fails to commit the transaction, the entire transaction is aborted.

Conflict-free replicated data types (CRDTs): CRDTs are data structures that are designed to ensure that the data remains consistent across all nodes. They are able to achieve this without the need for a central coordinator node, making them ideal for highly distributed systems.

Eventual consistency: In systems that require complex data synchronization and conflict resolution, eventual consistency may be a more appropriate model than strong consistency. Eventual consistency allows for updates to propagate through the system over time, eventually resulting in a consistent state across all nodes.

Distributed locking: Distributed locking can be used to ensure that only one node is able to update a particular piece of data at a time. This approach can be useful in situations where conflicts are likely to occur, and it can help to minimize the need for conflict resolution.

In conclusion, designing a system that requires complex data synchronization and conflict resolution can be challenging, but there are several strategies that can be employed to ensure that the data remains consistent and accurate across all nodes. These strategies include conflict detection and resolution, consistent data models, master-slave replication, two-phase commit, CRDTs, eventual consistency, and distributed locking.

5.11 What are some best practices for optimizing the performance of distributed databases and storage systems?

Optimizing the performance of distributed databases and storage systems is crucial for maintaining the efficiency and availability of a system. Here are some best practices to consider:

Choose the right database and storage technologies: There are various options available for distributed databases and storage systems such as SQL and NoSQL databases, object storage, block storage, and file storage. It is essential to choose the right technology that meets the requirements of the system and offers the best performance.

Scale horizontally: Horizontal scaling involves adding more servers or nodes to a system, which allows it to handle more data and traffic. Horizontal scaling can be achieved through techniques such as sharding, data partitioning, and load balancing.

Optimize data structures: The data structures used by a distributed system can significantly affect its performance. It is important to choose data structures that are optimized for distributed environments and can minimize the amount of data that needs to be transferred between nodes.

Use caching: Caching can significantly improve the performance of a distributed system by reducing the amount of time needed to retrieve data from a database or storage system. Caching can be implemented at different layers of the system, such as the application layer or the database layer.

Monitor and optimize queries: Optimizing queries is crucial for improving the performance of a distributed database. It is important to monitor the performance of queries and identify bottlenecks that can be optimized through techniques such as indexing, query optimization, and data denormalization.

Use compression and encryption: Compression and encryption can be used to reduce the size of data transmitted between nodes and ensure its security. However, it is important to balance the benefits of compression and encryption against their potential impact on system performance.

Manage data locality: Keeping data as close as possible to the processes that need it can significantly improve the performance of a distributed system. Techniques such as data partitioning, data replication, and data placement can be used to manage data locality.

Use distributed file systems: Distributed file systems such as Hadoop Distributed File System (HDFS) and Amazon S3 can be used to store and manage large amounts of data across multiple nodes. These systems offer features such as data replication, fault tolerance, and scalability, which can significantly improve the performance of a distributed system.

Monitor and optimize network performance: Network performance is a critical factor in the performance of a distributed system. It is important to monitor network performance and identify bottlenecks that can be optimized through techniques such as load balancing, network topology optimization, and protocol optimization.

By following these best practices, a distributed system can be optimized for performance, scalability, and reliability.

5.12   How do you design a system with support for complex access control and authentication mechanisms?

Designing a system with support for complex access control and authentication mechanisms is crucial for ensuring data security and privacy. Here are some best practices to consider:

Use a centralized authentication service: A centralized authentication service, such as OAuth or OpenID Connect, can simplify authentication and authorization across multiple systems and services. This approach enables users to log in once and access multiple applications and services without having to authenticate again.

Implement role-based access control: Role-based access control (RBAC) allows you to define access policies based on the role of the user. This approach ensures that users only have access to the data and resources they need to perform their job functions, reducing the risk of data breaches.

Use multi-factor authentication: Multi-factor authentication (MFA) provides an additional layer of security by requiring users to provide two or more pieces of evidence to authenticate their identity, such as a password and a code sent to their phone. This approach reduces the risk of unauthorized access even if the user's password is compromised.

Implement encryption: Encryption can protect sensitive data and prevent unauthorized access. Use end-to-end encryption for data in transit and encryption at rest for data stored in the system.

Monitor and log user activity: Monitoring and logging user activity can help detect and prevent unauthorized access or misuse of data. Use tools such as security information and event management (SIEM) systems to monitor user activity and generate alerts when suspicious activity is detected.

Regularly review and update access policies: Access policies should be reviewed and updated regularly to ensure they are up-to-date and aligned with the organization's security and compliance requirements.

Use secure coding practices: Secure coding practices, such as input validation and error handling, can prevent common security vulnerabilities, such as injection attacks and cross-site scripting (XSS) attacks.

In summary, designing a system with support for complex access control and authentication mechanisms requires a comprehensive approach that includes centralized authentication services, RBAC, MFA, encryption, monitoring and logging, regular policy reviews, and secure coding practices.

5.13   Can you discuss the challenges and best practices for implementing A/B testing and feature flagging in a large-scale system?

A/B testing and feature flagging are two common techniques used in software development to improve the user experience and test new features in production.

A/B testing involves comparing two different versions of a feature or design element to determine which performs better based on pre-defined metrics. For example, a company might test two different versions of a website's homepage to see which one results in more sign-ups or purchases. The results of the test can then be used to make informed decisions about which version to use going forward.

Feature flagging involves selectively enabling or disabling specific features or functionality within an application for different users or groups. This can be useful for testing new features or functionality without impacting all users, or for gradually rolling out new features to a subset of users before a wider release. Feature flags can also be used to quickly disable problematic features or to implement temporary workarounds.

Designing a system with support for A/B testing and feature flagging requires careful consideration of several factors. Here are some best practices to keep in mind:

Start with a plan: Before implementing A/B testing or feature flagging, it's important to have a clear plan in place for what you want to test or enable/disable, how you'll measure success, and how long you'll run the test. This will help ensure that you're collecting meaningful data and making informed decisions.

Use a feature flagging framework: There are many frameworks available for implementing feature flagging, such as LaunchDarkly or FeaturePeek. These frameworks provide an easy way to manage and control feature flags, as well as provide analytics and metrics for measuring their impact.

Keep things simple: It's easy to get carried away with feature flags and end up with a complex web of dependencies and conditions. Try to keep things simple by limiting the number of flags you use, and keeping them well-organized and documented.

Test early and often: A/B testing and feature flagging should be an ongoing process, not a one-time event. Continuously test and iterate on new features and designs to ensure that you're always improving the user experience and meeting business goals.

Monitor performance: A/B testing and feature flagging can have a significant impact on system performance, so it's important to monitor and measure their impact. Use analytics and monitoring tools to track performance metrics and identify any issues that may arise.

By following these best practices, you can design a system that supports A/B testing and feature flagging, and use these techniques to continually improve the user experience and achieve business goals.

5.14 How do you approach designing a system with support for real-time collaboration and conflict resolution?

Designing a system for real-time collaboration and conflict resolution involves a number of considerations to ensure that users can work together effectively and conflicts can be resolved seamlessly. Here are some key factors to consider:

Data model: The data model should be designed to support real-time updates and conflict resolution. This may involve breaking down data into smaller, more granular units that can be updated independently, as well as using techniques such as versioning to track changes and resolve conflicts.

Concurrency control: Concurrency control is a critical component of any system that supports real-time collaboration. Techniques such as optimistic concurrency control (OCC) can be used to ensure that conflicts are detected and resolved in real time, while still allowing multiple users to work on the same data simultaneously.

Communication protocols: The system must use communication protocols that support real-time collaboration, such as WebSocket or WebRTC, to enable low-latency updates and seamless collaboration.

Authorization and authentication: Effective authorization and authentication mechanisms are essential to ensure that users only have access to the data they are authorized to view or modify, and to prevent unauthorized access and data breaches.

Conflict resolution strategies: The system should provide conflict resolution strategies that enable users to resolve conflicts in real time, such as allowing users to merge conflicting changes or providing tools for manually resolving conflicts.

Offline access: The system should be designed to allow users to work offline and sync changes back to the server when they reconnect to the network.

User interface: The user interface should be designed to support real-time collaboration and conflict resolution, providing clear feedback to users when conflicts arise and enabling them to resolve conflicts quickly and easily.

Some examples of systems that require real-time collaboration and conflict resolution include collaborative document editing tools, project management systems, and online multiplayer games.

5.15   Can you discuss strategies for implementing a distributed, fault-tolerant, and scalable messaging system?

A messaging system is a fundamental building block for many distributed systems, enabling different services and components to communicate with each other asynchronously. Such a system should be able to handle a large number of messages, ensure reliability and durability of messages, and be able to scale as the system grows.

Here are some strategies for implementing a distributed, fault-tolerant, and scalable messaging system:

Message Queue: The message queue is the core component of the messaging system, responsible for storing messages until they are consumed by the intended recipients. A reliable and scalable message queue is essential to the success of the messaging system. Some popular message queue options include Apache Kafka, RabbitMQ, and Amazon SQS.

Load Balancing: As the messaging system grows, it may become necessary to distribute message processing across multiple nodes to avoid overloading a single node. Load balancing can be implemented using various techniques, such as round-robin, least connections, or IP hashing.

Replication: To ensure fault tolerance, the messaging system can replicate message queues across multiple nodes. If one node fails, another can take over the message processing.

Data Partitioning: To enable scalability, the messaging system can partition the message queue data across multiple nodes. This allows the system to scale horizontally by adding more nodes to the cluster.

Message Routing: Message routing is the process of directing messages to the correct recipient. The messaging system should be able to route messages based on various criteria, such as message content, recipient, or message priority.

Message Compression: To reduce message size and improve system performance, the messaging system can compress messages before storing or transmitting them.

Message Encryption: To ensure message security and prevent unauthorized access, the messaging system can encrypt messages before storing or transmitting them.

Monitoring and Alerting: It is essential to monitor the messaging system continuously and receive alerts when something goes wrong. This allows for rapid detection and resolution of any issues before they become critical.

Automated Scaling: To handle spikes in message traffic, the messaging system should be able to automatically scale up or down the number of nodes in the cluster based on message volume.

Message Expiration: To prevent message queues from growing indefinitely, the messaging system can implement message expiration policies to remove messages after a specified period.

In summary, a distributed, fault-tolerant, and scalable messaging system requires a robust message queue, load balancing, replication, data partitioning, message routing, compression, encryption, monitoring and alerting, automated scaling, and message expiration policies. These strategies can help ensure that the messaging system can handle a large volume of messages while providing reliable and durable message delivery.

5.16 What are some best practices for ensuring observability and monitoring in large-scale, distributed systems?

Observability and monitoring are critical aspects of building and maintaining large-scale, distributed systems. By observing system behavior and performance metrics, engineers can identify issues and optimize the system for maximum efficiency. In this answer, we will discuss some best practices for ensuring observability and monitoring in such systems.

Instrumentation: Instrumentation is the process of adding monitoring code to the system, which generates and sends telemetry data to a monitoring system. This telemetry data may include logs, metrics, and traces. A well-instrumented system provides visibility into its internal workings and enables engineers to diagnose issues effectively. For example, adding metrics to track response times, error rates, and throughput can help identify bottlenecks and performance issues.

Distributed Tracing: Distributed tracing is a technique that enables engineers to track a request's journey through a complex system of microservices, APIs, and other dependencies. By analyzing the data generated by distributed tracing, engineers can determine the root cause of an issue and understand the impact of changes to the system. OpenTracing and OpenCensus are two widely used distributed tracing frameworks.

Log Aggregation: A log aggregation system collects and stores logs generated by different components of the system in a central location. By consolidating logs from different sources, engineers can gain a holistic view of the system's behavior and identify issues more easily. Tools like Elasticsearch, Logstash, and Kibana (ELK) and Splunk are popular log aggregation solutions.

Alerting: Alerting is a critical part of monitoring. It notifies engineers when a system metric or performance threshold is exceeded. Engineers can set up alerts for various scenarios, such as when error rates exceed a certain percentage or when response times exceed a threshold. Alerting enables engineers to react quickly to issues and prevent system downtime.

Infrastructure Monitoring: Infrastructure monitoring involves monitoring the performance and health of the underlying infrastructure on which the system runs. This includes monitoring CPU, memory, and disk usage, network bandwidth, and other system-level metrics. Tools like Nagios, Zabbix, and Datadog can help monitor infrastructure.

Capacity Planning: Capacity planning involves predicting future resource requirements based on historical data and business projections. This enables engineers to proactively scale the system to handle increased demand, reducing the risk of downtime due to resource exhaustion.

Chaos Engineering: Chaos engineering is a practice that involves intentionally introducing failures into a system to test its resilience. By simulating real-world scenarios, engineers can identify potential issues and improve the system's resilience. Tools like Chaos Monkey and Gremlin can help engineers perform chaos engineering experiments.

In conclusion, ensuring observability and monitoring in large-scale, distributed systems requires a combination of instrumentation, distributed tracing, log aggregation, alerting, infrastructure monitoring, capacity planning, and chaos engineering. By adopting these best practices, engineers can gain visibility into the system's behavior and diagnose issues effectively, improving the system's reliability, availability, and scalability.

5.17   How do you design a system with support for dynamic scaling, including auto-scaling and scale-in mechanisms?

Designing a system with support for dynamic scaling is critical for modern applications that need to handle variable workloads and sudden spikes in traffic. Here are some strategies for achieving this:

Horizontal scaling: Horizontal scaling is the process of adding more instances of the application to the existing infrastructure to handle the increased load. This can be achieved by adding more servers or instances of the application in a cloud environment, where auto-scaling groups can dynamically add or remove instances based on demand. For example, in Amazon Web Services, you can use Elastic Load Balancing to distribute incoming traffic to multiple EC2 instances running your application.

Vertical scaling: Vertical scaling is the process of adding more resources to an individual instance of the application, such as increasing the CPU or memory. This can be useful in cases where a single instance can handle the traffic but needs more resources to do so. However, vertical scaling has its limitations and can only go so far in terms of scalability.

Stateless architecture: A stateless architecture is one where each request is independent and doesn't depend on any previous request or state. This allows for easier horizontal scaling since new instances can be added or removed without affecting the overall state of the application. For example, a stateless web application can use a load balancer to distribute requests evenly among multiple instances.

Load testing: Load testing is the process of simulating high levels of traffic to the application to see how it handles the load. By performing load testing, you can identify bottlenecks and performance issues before they become a problem. Load testing can also help you determine the optimal number of instances needed to handle the expected load.

Auto-scaling: Auto-scaling is the process of automatically adding or removing instances based on the demand. This is typically done using a metric such as CPU usage, network traffic, or other performance indicators. Auto-scaling can be done manually or automatically based on predefined rules.

Scale-in mechanisms: Scale-in mechanisms are the processes used to remove instances that are no longer needed. For example, you can set up a rule to remove instances when CPU usage falls below a certain threshold. Scale-in mechanisms are important because they help to reduce costs by removing unnecessary resources when they are no longer needed.

Overall, designing a system with support for dynamic scaling requires careful planning and consideration of the application's requirements and expected workload. By following best practices and using tools and services designed for scalability, you can create a system that can handle changing demands and maintain performance under heavy load.

5.18 Can you discuss the challenges and best practices for implementing machine learning models in a distributed system?

Implementing machine learning (ML) models in a distributed system poses unique challenges due to the computational requirements of ML algorithms and the need for efficient data processing. Some of the key challenges in designing such a system include:

Data Storage and Retrieval: Storing and retrieving large datasets is a significant challenge for distributed machine learning systems. Efficient data storage and retrieval mechanisms are needed to ensure that data can be processed quickly, even when it is spread across multiple nodes.

Data Preprocessing and Feature Extraction: Data preprocessing and feature extraction are essential steps in machine learning that involve preparing data for analysis. These steps need to be efficient and optimized to avoid delays in the training and evaluation of ML models.

Model Training and Tuning: Training and tuning ML models can be a computationally intensive task, especially when dealing with large datasets or complex models. Distributed systems need to be designed to handle the high computational requirements of these tasks.

Model Deployment and Management: Once an ML model has been trained, it needs to be deployed and managed effectively. This includes monitoring the model's performance, ensuring that it is up-to-date, and scaling it as needed to meet changing demands.

To overcome these challenges, some best practices for implementing machine learning models in a distributed system include:

Data Partitioning: Partitioning data across multiple nodes can help distribute the computational load and enable faster processing. This can be achieved using techniques such as data sharding, where data is split into smaller chunks and distributed across multiple nodes.

Parallel Processing: Parallel processing can help improve the performance of ML algorithms by enabling multiple nodes to work on the same task simultaneously. Techniques such as map-reduce and parallel batch processing can be used to achieve this.

Model Compression and Optimization: ML models can be compressed and optimized to reduce their size and computational requirements. This can help reduce the amount of processing required and enable faster model training and evaluation.

Auto-Scaling: Auto-scaling mechanisms can be used to automatically adjust the number of resources allocated to a distributed system based on demand. This can help ensure that the system can handle changing workloads and avoid unnecessary resource consumption.

Monitoring and Logging: Monitoring and logging are critical for ensuring the reliability and performance of a distributed machine learning system. Real-time monitoring can help detect issues as they occur, while logging can be used to track the performance of the system over time.

By following these best practices, developers can design and implement distributed machine learning systems that are efficient, reliable, and scalable, and can deliver accurate and actionable insights from large datasets.

5.19 How do you approach capacity planning and performance testing for large-scale, distributed systems?

Capacity planning and performance testing are critical aspects of designing large-scale, distributed systems. Capacity planning involves estimating the resources required to meet future demand, while performance testing involves validating the system's performance under various conditions. Here are some strategies for approaching these tasks:

Understand the system's requirements: Before planning for capacity and testing performance, it's important to understand the system's requirements in terms of expected usage, user base, and expected growth. This information can help guide capacity planning and performance testing efforts.

Define performance metrics: Performance metrics such as response time, throughput, and error rate can help define the system's performance requirements. These metrics can be used as benchmarks during performance testing and can help identify potential bottlenecks.

Conduct load testing: Load testing involves simulating the expected load on the system to validate its performance under different conditions. This can include testing the system's ability to handle peak loads, as well as its performance under steady-state conditions.

Use stress testing: Stress testing involves pushing the system beyond its expected limits to identify failure points and validate the system's resilience. This can help identify potential bottlenecks and ensure that the system can handle unexpected spikes in traffic.

Leverage cloud services: Cloud services such as AWS, Azure, and Google Cloud provide tools and services for capacity planning and performance testing. These services can help simulate traffic and load on the system, as well as provide real-time monitoring and analytics.

Monitor system performance: Continuous monitoring of system performance can help identify issues and bottlenecks in real-time. This can help with capacity planning efforts by identifying when additional resources may be required to meet future demand.

Optimize system resources: Optimizing system resources such as memory, CPU, and network bandwidth can help improve system performance and reduce resource usage. This can include using caching mechanisms, optimizing database queries, and compressing data.

By considering these strategies, designers can ensure that their distributed systems are able to meet expected demand and perform optimally under various conditions.

5.20   What are some best practices for designing and implementing a robust disaster recovery strategy in a distributed system?

Disaster recovery is a crucial aspect of any large-scale distributed system design, as it involves ensuring that the system can quickly recover and resume normal operations in the event of a catastrophic failure or outage. Here are some best practices for designing and implementing a robust disaster recovery strategy in a distributed system:

Define Recovery Point Objectives (RPO) and Recovery Time Objectives (RTO): These are two key metrics that define the maximum acceptable data loss and downtime, respectively, in the event of a disaster. It's important to define these metrics upfront and design the disaster recovery plan accordingly.

Use a multi-region architecture: By replicating data and services across multiple regions, you can ensure that the system remains available and operational even in the event of a region-wide outage.

Implement automated failover mechanisms: Automated failover mechanisms, such as DNS failover or load balancer failover, can help to quickly redirect traffic to healthy instances in the event of a failure.

Regularly test the disaster recovery plan: It's important to regularly test the disaster recovery plan to ensure that it is working as expected and that the RPO and RTO metrics are being met.

Implement backups: Backups are essential for restoring data in the event of a disaster. It's important to regularly backup data and ensure that the backups are stored in a secure and easily accessible location.

Use redundant hardware and infrastructure: Using redundant hardware and infrastructure, such as redundant power supplies, network connections, and storage systems, can help to minimize the risk of hardware failures.

Implement access controls and security measures: Disaster recovery plans should include access controls and security measures to prevent unauthorized access to the system or data.

Define roles and responsibilities: It's important to define roles and responsibilities for disaster recovery, including who is responsible for implementing the plan, who is responsible for testing the plan, and who is responsible for communicating with stakeholders in the event of a disaster.

Overall, a robust disaster recovery plan requires careful planning, regular testing, and the implementation of redundant systems and security measures to ensure that the system can quickly recover and resume normal operations in the event of a disaster.

Chapter 6

Guru

6.1 Can you discuss advanced strategies for achieving linearizability and serializability in distributed databases?

Linearizability and serializability are two important properties of distributed databases that ensure the consistency and correctness of data across all nodes in the system. Achieving these properties can be challenging in large-scale distributed systems due to the presence of concurrent requests and the need for high availability and fault tolerance.

Linearizability refers to the property of a system where all operations appear to occur instantaneously, in a total order. This means that every operation should appear to take place at a single point in time, and all nodes in the system see the same sequence of operations. For example, consider a distributed system that stores bank account balances. If two people simultaneously attempt to withdraw money from the same account, the system must ensure that the balance is updated in a way that appears atomic to all nodes, regardless of which node processed the requests.

Serializability, on the other hand, refers to the property of a system where the execution of a set of concurrent transactions is equivalent to executing them one at a time in some order. This ensures that the result of executing concurrent transactions is the same as executing them sequentially, which is essential for maintaining data consistency. For example, consider a distributed system that allows users to transfer money between bank accounts. If two users initiate transfers simultaneously, the system must ensure that the transfers are executed in a way that preserves the consistency of the balances in all accounts.

To achieve linearizability and serializability in distributed databases, several advanced strategies can be used:

Two-phase commit (2PC): This is a protocol that ensures atomicity and consistency of distributed transactions by coordinating all nodes involved in the transaction. The protocol involves a coordinator that initiates the transaction and communicates with all participants to commit or abort the transaction. 2PC guarantees that all nodes either commit or abort the transaction, ensuring that the transaction is atomic and consistent across all nodes.

Multi-version concurrency control (MVCC): MVCC is a technique used to manage concurrency in a distributed database by allowing multiple versions of the same data to exist simultaneously. Each version of the data is associated with a timestamp, which ensures that all nodes can see a consistent view of the data at any point in time. MVCC is used in many distributed databases, including Apache Cassandra.

Consensus algorithms: Consensus algorithms are used to achieve agreement among a group of nodes in a distributed system, such as in the case of leader election or data replication. Popular consensus algorithms include Paxos and Raft, which are used in many distributed databases, including Apache ZooKeeper and etcd.

Vector clocks: Vector clocks are used to track the causal relationships between events in a distributed system. Each node maintains a vector clock that represents the sequence of events seen by that node, which can be used to resolve conflicts and maintain consistency across all nodes.

Conflict-free replicated data types (CRDTs): CRDTs are a class of data structures that can be replicated across multiple nodes in a distributed system, ensuring that the replicas converge to the same state over time. CRDTs are designed to handle concurrent updates to the same data, ensuring that the updates are eventually consistent across all nodes.

In conclusion, achieving linearizability and serializability in distributed databases requires careful consideration of the underlying data model, concurrency control mechanisms, and consensus algorithms. Advanced strategies such as 2PC, MVCC, consensus algorithms, vector clocks, and CRDTs can be used to achieve these properties in a distributed system, ensuring consistency and correctness across all nodes.

6.2 How do you design a distributed system with support for advanced data processing, such as graph processing or semantic analysis?

Designing a distributed system with support for advanced data processing involves several challenges, including data partitioning, data consistency, and processing efficiency. Here are some strategies that can be used to address these challenges:

Data partitioning: Partitioning data involves dividing large data sets into smaller, more manageable pieces that can be stored and processed on different nodes in the system. Some common partitioning strategies include range partitioning, hash partitioning, and list partitioning. For example, in a graph processing system, nodes and edges can be partitioned based on their attributes or identifiers, such as the node ID or edge weight.

Data consistency: Maintaining data consistency across different nodes in a distributed system is crucial for ensuring correct and accurate results. There are several consistency models, including strong consistency, eventual consistency, and causal consistency, each with its trade-offs in terms of availability, latency, and complexity. For example, a graph processing system may require strong consistency for maintaining accurate results, whereas an analytics system may tolerate eventual consistency to ensure high availability.

Processing efficiency: Advanced data processing often involves complex algorithms that can be computationally expensive. To achieve high processing efficiency, several techniques can be used, such as parallel processing, data caching, and data compression. For example, a distributed system for semantic analysis may use parallel processing to divide the analysis task into smaller, more manageable parts that can be processed simultaneously on different nodes.

Data storage: Advanced data processing often requires specialized data storage systems that can handle the unique data structures and processing requirements of the application. For example, a graph processing system may use a specialized graph database that can efficiently store and process graph data.

Distributed computation frameworks: Several distributed computation frameworks, such as Apache Hadoop and Apache Spark, can be used to build distributed systems with support for advanced data processing. These frameworks provide high-level abstractions for data processing, such as MapReduce, and handle many of the low-level details of distributed computation, such as fault tolerance and data partitioning.

In summary, designing a distributed system with support for advanced data processing involves several challenges, including data partitioning, data consistency, and processing efficiency. However, by using techniques such as data partitioning, data consistency models, processing efficiency strategies, specialized data storage systems, and distributed computation frameworks, it is possible to build robust and scalable systems for advanced data processing such as graph processing or semantic analysis.

6.3 Can you discuss the challenges and best practices for implementing geo-replication and data locality in global-scale systems?

Geo-replication is the process of copying data from one location to another in order to ensure data is available in the event of a disaster or failure. It is a crucial technique for ensuring high availability and disaster recovery in large-scale distributed systems. However, implementing geo-replication in a global-scale system can present a number of challenges, including network latency, data consistency, and data locality.

One of the biggest challenges with implementing geo-replication in a global-scale system is network latency. As data needs to be transferred across large geographic distances, network latency can significantly impact the performance and availability of the system. This can be addressed by implementing techniques such as data compression and optimization, and using content delivery networks (CDNs) to cache frequently accessed data closer to the end user.

Another challenge is maintaining data consistency across multiple locations. As data is replicated across different locations, ensuring that all copies of the data are consistent becomes increasingly difficult. To address this, distributed systems can use techniques such as multi-version concurrency control (MVCC) or conflict-free replicated data types (CRDTs) to ensure that all data copies are consistent with each other.

Data locality is another important consideration in global-scale systems. In order to ensure optimal performance, it is important to store data as close as possible to the users who will be accessing it. This can be achieved by using techniques such as sharding, which involves partitioning data across different servers based on specific criteria, such as geographic location or user demographics.

In addition to these challenges, there are also a number of best practices for implementing geo-replication and data locality in global-scale systems. These include:

Designing for failure: Global-scale systems need to be designed with failure in mind. This means implementing techniques such as automatic failover, redundant storage, and backup and recovery procedures.

Minimizing data transfer: As data transfer is a major bottleneck in global-scale systems, it is important to minimize the amount of data that needs to be transferred. This can be achieved through techniques such as delta compression, which only transfers the changes made to a file rather than the entire file.

Prioritizing data: Not all data is created equal, and it is important to prioritize data based on its criticality and importance. This can be achieved by implementing data tiering, which involves storing high-priority data in faster and more accessible storage, and lower-priority data in slower, cheaper storage.

Monitoring and testing: Finally, it is important to continually monitor and test global-scale systems to ensure that they are performing optimally and meeting the needs of end users. This involves implementing robust monitoring and testing procedures, and using analytics tools to identify areas for improvement.

Overall, implementing geo-replication and data locality in global-scale systems presents a number of challenges, but with the right techniques and best practices, these challenges can be overcome to ensure that data is available and accessible to users around the world.

6.4 What are some advanced techniques for optimizing query performance in distributed databases, such as materialized views or query rewriting?

Distributed databases are designed to store data across multiple nodes, making it possible to handle larger datasets and provide high availability and scalability. However, querying such a distributed database can present several challenges, including increased network latency and the need to coordinate the data across nodes.

Here are some advanced techniques for optimizing query performance in distributed databases:

Materialized Views: A materialized view is a precomputed query result that is stored and maintained as a table in the database. Materialized views can improve query performance by reducing the number of joins and aggregations required to answer a query. They are particularly useful for queries that involve complex joins and aggregations or queries that are executed frequently.

For example, suppose you have a distributed database that stores information about customers and their orders. You could create a materialized view that computes the total revenue for each customer, which would make it easier to answer queries such as "Which customers have the highest revenue?".

Query Rewriting: Query rewriting involves transforming a query into a semantically equivalent form that can be executed more efficiently. This technique is particularly useful for optimizing queries that involve distributed data.

For example, suppose you have a distributed database that stores information about products and their sales. You could rewrite a query that involves a join between the product and sales tables by first filtering the sales table to include only the relevant products and then performing the join. This approach would reduce the amount of data that needs to be transferred across nodes, improving query performance.

Sharding: Sharding involves partitioning data across multiple nodes based on a specific criterion, such as customer ID or geographic location. This technique can improve query performance by reducing the amount of data that needs to be searched to answer a query.

For example, suppose you have a distributed database that stores information about products and customers across multiple nodes. By sharding the data based on customer ID, you can ensure that all the data for a particular customer is stored on a single node, making it easier to answer queries that involve that customer.

Distributed Indexing: Distributed indexing involves creating and maintaining indexes across multiple nodes in the database. This technique can improve query performance by reducing the number of nodes that need to be searched to answer a query.

For example, suppose you have a distributed database that stores information about products and their sales across multiple nodes. By creating an index on the sales table that is distributed across all the nodes, you can ensure that the query engine only needs to search the relevant nodes to answer a query.

In summary, optimizing query performance in distributed databases requires a combination of techniques, including materialized views, query rewriting, sharding, and distributed indexing. By carefully selecting the appropriate techniques for your particular use case, you can achieve significant improvements in query performance and overall system efficiency.

6.5   How do you design a system with support for advanced consistency guarantees, such as snapshot isolation or external consistency?

When designing a distributed system, one of the key considerations is the level of consistency that is required. Different consistency models offer different guarantees about the state of the system, and the choice of model depends on the specific needs of the application.

Two advanced consistency models that are commonly used in distributed systems are snapshot isolation and external consistency.

Snapshot isolation is a consistency model that guarantees that each transaction sees a consistent snapshot of the database at a specific point in time. Under this model, each transaction executes as if it were the only transaction in the system, and is isolated from the effects of other concurrent transactions until it is committed. This ensures that each transaction sees a consistent view of the data, without the risk of reading uncommitted data or writing data that is subsequently overwritten by another transaction.

External consistency, on the other hand, guarantees that the system as a whole maintains consistency across all replicas, even in the presence of failures or network partitions. This consistency model requires careful coordination between nodes to ensure that updates are propagated in a consistent and reliable way, and that all nodes eventually converge to a consistent state.

To design a system with support for snapshot isolation, one approach is to use a database that supports this consistency model natively, such as PostgreSQL or Oracle. Alternatively, it is possible to implement snapshot isolation using a distributed transaction protocol such as Two-Phase Commit (2PC), or by using a distributed caching layer that provides snapshot isolation guarantees.

To design a system with support for external consistency, it is important to carefully consider the replication and synchronization mechanisms that will be used to ensure that all nodes eventually converge to a consistent state. This may involve using a consensus algorithm such as Paxos or Raft to coordinate updates, or using a distributed database that provides built-in support for external consistency.

Overall, the choice of consistency model will depend on the specific needs of the application, and the trade-offs between consistency, availability, and partition tolerance that are acceptable for the system.

6.6 Can you discuss the challenges and best practices for implementing advanced data management techniques, such as multi-master replication or distributed transactions?

Implementing advanced data management techniques in distributed systems is a complex task that involves various challenges and best practices. Here are some key points to consider:

Multi-master replication: Multi-master replication is the process of replicating data across multiple nodes in a distributed system. One of the main challenges in implementing multi-master replication is managing conflicts that arise when two nodes try to modify the same piece of data simultaneously. To address this, systems can use conflict resolution strategies such as last write wins or vector clocks. Additionally, to improve performance, systems can use asynchronous replication where updates are propagated to other nodes in the background.

Distributed transactions: Distributed transactions are transactions that involve multiple nodes in a distributed system. The main challenge in implementing distributed transactions is maintaining consistency across all nodes. Two-phase commit is a common technique used to ensure that all nodes commit or roll back a transaction atomically. However, two-phase commit can be slow and can result in blocking if one of the nodes fails to respond. Optimistic concurrency control can be used as an alternative approach where each node maintains its own copy of the data and resolves conflicts when necessary.

Consistency models: Consistency models define the level of consistency that a distributed system guarantees. Strong consistency guarantees that all nodes see the same state of the data at the same time. Weak consistency allows for temporary inconsistencies but guarantees eventual consistency. External consistency is a stronger guarantee than weak consistency but weaker than strong consistency. The choice of consistency model depends on the specific requirements of the system and the trade-offs between consistency, availability, and partition tolerance.

Data partitioning: Data partitioning is the process of dividing data into smaller subsets to enable parallel processing. One of the main challenges in implementing data partitioning is determining the optimal partitioning scheme. Systems can use various partitioning strategies such as range partitioning or hash partitioning. Additionally, systems can use techniques such as consistent hashing to ensure that data is evenly distributed across nodes.

Data compression: Data compression is the process of reducing the size of data to improve performance and reduce storage requirements. One of the challenges in implementing data compression is selecting the optimal compression algorithm. Systems can use various compression algorithms such as LZO, Snappy, or Gzip, depending on the data characteristics and the performance requirements.

In summary, implementing advanced data management techniques in distributed systems requires careful consideration of various challenges and best practices such as managing conflicts, choosing the right consistency model, optimizing data partitioning, selecting the optimal compression algorithm, and implementing efficient distributed transactions.

6.7 What are some advanced strategies for achieving fault-tolerance and self-healing in large-scale, distributed systems?

As distributed systems grow larger and more complex, the likelihood of individual components failing increases. Ensuring fault-tolerance and self-healing in these systems is critical to maintaining system availability and reliability. Here are some advanced strategies for achieving fault-tolerance and self-healing in large-scale, distributed systems:

Replication and redundancy: One of the most effective strategies for achieving fault-tolerance is through replication and redundancy. By replicating data and services across multiple nodes or data centers, the system can continue to function even if individual components fail. This approach is used extensively in modern cloud architectures, such as AWS or GCP, where redundancy is built into the underlying infrastructure.

Monitoring and alerting: Another key component of fault-tolerance is monitoring and alerting. By setting up monitoring tools and dashboards, teams can detect issues before they become critical and take proactive measures to address them. For example, setting up alerts for high CPU usage or memory usage can help identify performance issues before they impact users.

Automated recovery: A critical component of self-healing is automated recovery. By implementing self-healing mechanisms, such as automatic failover or automatic scaling, the system can respond to failures without human intervention. For example, if a node fails, an automated failover mechanism can redirect traffic to a healthy node, ensuring uninterrupted service.

Chaos engineering: Chaos engineering is a practice that involves intentionally introducing failure into a system to test its resilience. By simulating failure scenarios, teams can identify weaknesses in the system and take steps to address them. For example, by shutting down a database node or network switch, teams can test how the system responds and identify potential issues.

Microservices architecture: Microservices architecture is an approach to building distributed systems where applications are broken down into smaller, independent services that can be developed, deployed, and scaled independently. This approach allows teams to isolate failures to individual services and prevent them from affecting the entire system.

Immutable infrastructure: Immutable infrastructure is an approach to system design where infrastructure components are never modified directly. Instead, new components are created with each deployment, ensuring that the system is always in a consistent, known state. This approach can simplify recovery and make it easier to roll back changes in the event of a failure.

Overall, achieving fault-tolerance and self-healing in large-scale, distributed systems requires a combination of design patterns, tooling, and cultural practices. By implementing these advanced strategies, teams can build systems that are more resilient, reliable, and responsive to changing conditions.

6.8 How do you approach designing a distributed system with support for advanced analytics, such as machine learning or data mining?

Designing a distributed system with support for advanced analytics requires careful consideration of several factors such as data processing, storage, and analysis. The following are some of the key points to keep in mind:

Data ingestion and processing: In order to perform analytics on data, it needs to be ingested into the system and processed. Depending on the data sources and volume, this can be a complex process that requires careful design. Techniques such as parallel processing, stream processing, and batch processing can be used to efficiently handle large volumes of data.

Data storage: The data that is ingested and processed needs to be stored in a format that is optimized for analytics. This can involve the use of specialized data stores such as data warehouses or data lakes. The choice of data store will depend on the nature of the data, the analytics requirements, and the performance and scalability needs of the system.

Analytics processing: Once the data is stored, it needs to be analyzed using techniques such as machine learning or data mining. This requires specialized tools and frameworks that can process data in parallel across distributed nodes. Popular tools for analytics processing include Apache Spark, Apache Hadoop, and TensorFlow.

Data visualization and reporting: The insights gained from analytics processing need to be presented to users in a meaningful way. This can involve the use of interactive dashboards, reports, or visualizations. The choice of tools and techniques for data visualization will depend on the requirements of the system and the preferences of the users.

Performance and scalability: A system that is designed for advanced analytics needs to be able to handle large volumes of data and process it efficiently. This requires careful consideration of factors such as network bandwidth, compute resources, and storage capacity. Techniques such as sharding, load balancing, and caching can be used to improve system performance and scalability.

Security and privacy: Finally, a system that is designed for advanced analytics needs to ensure the security and privacy of the data being processed. This can involve the use of techniques such as encryption, access control, and data anonymization.

To illustrate, let's consider the example of a large e-commerce website that wants to design a system to perform advanced analytics on customer behavior. The system would need to ingest data from multiple sources such as web logs, clickstream data, and transaction data. This data would then be processed using stream processing techniques such as Apache Kafka, and stored in a data lake using a distributed file system such as Hadoop. The analytics processing would be performed using a framework such as Apache Spark or TensorFlow, and the results would be presented to users using interactive dashboards or reports. The system would be designed to handle large volumes of data and scale horizontally using techniques such as sharding and load balancing. Finally, the system would ensure the security and privacy of the data being processed using techniques such as encryption and access control.

6.9 Can you discuss the challenges and best practices for implementing distributed machine learning and model serving in large-scale systems?

Distributed machine learning and model serving are essential components of modern large-scale systems that require real-time, intelligent decision-making. These techniques enable the system to learn from data, make predictions, and take actions in a distributed and scalable way. However, implementing these techniques in large-scale systems can be challenging due to several reasons, such as the large volume of data, distributed nature of the system, and the need to maintain consistency and accuracy of the models.

Here are some of the challenges and best practices for implementing distributed machine learning and model serving:

Challenges:

Data consistency and distribution: In a distributed system, the data used for training the machine learning models is often distributed across multiple nodes. Ensuring data consistency and distribution is a critical challenge as it affects the accuracy and quality of the models.

Scalability and performance: Distributed machine learning and model serving require a high level of scalability and performance to handle the large volume of data and requests in real-time.

Model management and versioning: Managing and versioning machine learning models in a distributed system is a challenging task. The models need to be trained, validated, and updated across multiple nodes while ensuring consistency and accuracy.

Security and privacy: Ensuring the security and privacy of the data used in distributed machine learning and model serving is a crucial challenge. The data needs to be protected from unauthorized access and potential attacks.

Best Practices:

Data preprocessing and cleansing: Preprocessing and cleansing the data before training the machine learning models is critical to ensure consistency and accuracy. This includes removing missing values, outlier detection, and normalization.

Model selection and training: Selecting the appropriate machine learning algorithm and training the models on a representative dataset is essential for accurate predictions. This includes optimizing hyperparameters, selecting appropriate feature sets, and using cross-validation techniques.

Model serving and management: Implementing a robust model serving and management system is critical for the scalability and performance of the system. This includes using distributed caching, load balancing, and parallel processing techniques.

Data partitioning and distribution: Partitioning and distributing the data across multiple nodes in the system is essential for scalability and performance. This includes using techniques such as sharding, replication, and data partitioning.

Consistency and accuracy: Ensuring consistency and accuracy of the models across all nodes in the system is critical. This includes using techniques such as consensus algorithms, distributed locking, and version control.

Security and privacy: Ensuring the security and privacy of the data used in distributed machine learning and model serving is a critical factor. This includes using techniques such as data encryption, access control, and secure communication protocols.

In conclusion, implementing distributed machine learning and model serving in large-scale systems requires careful consideration of several factors, such as data consistency, scalability, model management, and security. Following best practices such as data preprocessing and cleansing, model selection and training, model serving and management, data partitioning and distribution, consistency and accuracy, and security and privacy can help ensure the success of these techniques in large-scale systems.

6.10 What are some advanced techniques for optimizing the performance and efficiency of data storage and retrieval, such as data compression or tiered storage?

As data volumes continue to grow, optimizing the performance and efficiency of data storage and retrieval becomes increasingly important in large-scale systems. Here are some advanced techniques that can be used to achieve this:

Data Compression: Data compression is a technique that reduces the size of data by encoding it in a more compact form. This can significantly reduce storage requirements and improve I/O performance. One example of this is using columnar storage, which stores data in columns rather than rows, enabling better compression.

Tiered Storage: Tiered storage involves using different types of storage media (e.g., SSDs, HDDs, tape) to store data based on its importance or frequency of access. This can reduce costs by using cheaper storage media for less critical data and improve performance by using faster storage for frequently accessed data.

Data Partitioning: Data partitioning involves dividing data into smaller, more manageable chunks that can be stored and processed in parallel. This can improve performance by reducing the amount of data that needs to be processed at any given time.

Caching: Caching involves storing frequently accessed data in a cache for faster retrieval. This can improve performance by reducing the amount of I/O required to access data.

Indexing: Indexing involves creating indexes on data to enable faster searching and retrieval. This can significantly improve the performance of queries that search for specific data.

Data Sharding: Data sharding involves horizontally partitioning data across multiple nodes in a cluster. This can improve performance by enabling parallel processing and reducing the amount of data that needs to be transmitted across the network.

Data Deduplication: Data deduplication involves identifying and removing duplicate data to reduce storage requirements. This can improve performance by reducing the amount of data that needs to be processed and transmitted.

By using these techniques, large-scale systems can improve the performance and efficiency of data storage and retrieval, enabling faster processing and reducing costs. However, it's important to carefully evaluate the trade-offs involved in each technique and choose the ones that are most appropriate for the specific system and its requirements.

6.11 How do you design a distributed system with support for advanced security and privacy requirements, such as zero-knowledge proofs or secure multi-party computation?

Designing a distributed system with advanced security and privacy requirements is a challenging task. Here are some strategies and considerations to keep in mind when building such a system:

Threat modeling: It's essential to identify potential threats and vulnerabilities that can compromise the security and privacy of the system. Conducting a threat modeling exercise helps identify potential weaknesses and guides the design of security and privacy controls.

Secure communication: The communication between the different components of the distributed system must be secure. Encryption, authentication, and authorization mechanisms are essential to ensure that only authorized parties can access the data.

Access control: Access control mechanisms are critical to ensuring that only authorized users can access and manipulate data. Role-based access control (RBAC), attribute-based access control (ABAC), and mandatory access control (MAC) are some popular access control models that can be implemented.

Encryption: Encryption can be used to protect data both in transit and at rest. Techniques such as homomorphic encryption, differential privacy, and zero-knowledge proofs can be used to provide advanced privacy guarantees.

Data anonymization: Anonymization techniques such as k-anonymity, l-diversity, and t-closeness can be used to ensure that sensitive information is protected while still allowing useful analysis.

Multi-party computation: Multi-party computation (MPC) is a cryptographic technique that allows multiple parties to compute a function without revealing their inputs. MPC can be used to enable secure collaboration between parties without compromising privacy.

Auditing and monitoring: It's essential to monitor and audit the system to detect and respond to security incidents quickly. Logging and monitoring mechanisms should be put in place to detect unusual behavior or suspicious activities.

Compliance: Compliance with industry standards and regulations such as GDPR, HIPAA, or PCI-DSS is crucial when dealing with sensitive data. The system should be designed to comply with these standards and regulations.

Examples of systems that require advanced security and privacy requirements include healthcare systems, financial systems, and government systems. In healthcare systems, patient data is highly sensitive and must be protected. Financial systems deal with sensitive financial data, and government systems deal with sensitive national security information.

Overall, designing a distributed system with advanced security and privacy requirements is a complex task that requires careful consideration of the potential threats and vulnerabilities, as well as the design of appropriate security and privacy controls.

6.12 Can you discuss the challenges and best practices for implementing advanced event-driven architectures and stream processing in large-scale systems?

Event-driven architectures (EDA) and stream processing have become popular approaches for designing large-scale, distributed systems that require real-time data processing and analysis.

EDA is an architectural pattern in which events, or changes in state, trigger a flow of data through a series of loosely coupled components that can react to and produce events. The components in the system are connected via event channels, which allow for the decoupling of the producers and consumers of events. In an event-driven architecture, events can be generated by internal system processes, user interactions, or external sources such as sensors or third-party services. These events are then processed by the system's components, which can perform tasks such as data transformation, aggregation, filtering, or triggering additional events.

Stream processing, on the other hand, refers to the real-time processing of data streams, which are continuous and potentially infinite sequences of data records. Stream processing allows for the processing of data as it arrives, rather than waiting for a batch to accumulate before processing. This approach is particularly useful in scenarios such as real-time analytics, fraud detection, or monitoring systems where timely responses to data changes are critical.

Here are some key challenges and best practices for implementing advanced event-driven architectures and stream processing in large-scale systems:

Choosing the right event source: Selecting the appropriate event source is crucial for the effectiveness of the event-driven architecture. The source should generate events that are relevant to the system's use case and provide a reliable and scalable mechanism for delivering events. For example, a large-scale e-commerce platform might use order processing systems as an event source to trigger downstream actions such as inventory updates, billing, or shipping notifications.

Ensuring data consistency: Maintaining consistency and correctness of data across the event-driven system can be challenging, especially when dealing with distributed systems and eventual consistency models. A common solution is to use an event log, which provides a persistent, immutable, and ordered record of all events in the system. The event log can act as a single source of truth and provide the necessary guarantees for data consistency and accuracy.

Scaling the system: As the system grows, scaling becomes a critical factor in ensuring that the event-driven architecture can handle the volume of incoming events and process them in real-time. This can be achieved through techniques such as partitioning the event stream, horizontal scaling of components, or using specialized stream processing frameworks such as Apache Kafka or Apache Flink.

Ensuring fault-tolerance: In an event-driven architecture, failures are inevitable, and the system should be able to recover from them quickly and seamlessly. Techniques such as redundancy, replication, and data backup can help ensure that the system remains available even in the face of failures.

Monitoring and observability: As the system becomes more complex, monitoring and observability become crucial for understanding system behavior and identifying potential issues. Implementing effective monitoring and observability requires instrumenting the system with metrics, logs, and traces, and using tools such as dashboards, alerts, and anomaly detection to gain insights into the system's health.

In summary, implementing advanced event-driven architectures and stream processing in large-scale systems requires careful consideration of the event source, data consistency, scalability, fault-tolerance, and monitoring. By following best practices in these areas, it's possible to build systems that can process vast amounts of data in real-time and provide valuable insights and actions to users.

6.13 What are some advanced strategies for handling data versioning and schema evolution in distributed systems?

Handling data versioning and schema evolution in distributed systems is a challenging task, especially as the system evolves and grows over time. When making changes to a system, it's essential to consider how those changes will affect the data that's stored and how the system will continue to function.

Here are some advanced strategies for handling data versioning and schema evolution in distributed systems:

Versioning of data and schema: To manage schema evolution and data versioning, a system should maintain different versions of the schema and data. As new features are added or the system evolves, changes to the schema can be made and rolled out incrementally, with old versions of the data and schema maintained for backward compatibility.

Compatibility of data and schema: The system should ensure that the new schema is compatible with the old data, and vice versa. This is particularly important when rolling out schema changes to large-scale systems, as changes that break compatibility can cause the system to fail.

Data migration: Data migration is the process of transferring data from one system to another or between different versions of the same system. When making changes to a system's schema, data migration is an essential consideration, as it's necessary to ensure that the data is correctly migrated to the new schema and that any necessary data transformations or conversions are applied.

Data validation: When making schema changes or migrating data, it's crucial to ensure that the data is validated and any errors are detected and corrected. Data validation can be a time-consuming process, but it's necessary to ensure the integrity and accuracy of the data.

Change management: Change management is an essential aspect of managing schema evolution and data versioning. As the system evolves, changes to the data and schema should be made through a formal change management process that includes testing, validation, and documentation.

Testing and validation: Testing and validation are critical to ensure that the system continues to function correctly after changes to the schema or data have been made. This includes testing the new schema and data versions, validating the data, and performing any necessary data transformations or conversions.

Rollback and recovery: In the event of a failure or error, the system should be able to roll back to the previous version of the schema or data and recover any lost or corrupted data. This requires a robust backup and recovery strategy and the ability to quickly restore the system to its previous state.

In summary, managing data versioning and schema evolution in distributed systems requires careful planning and consideration of the system's design and architecture. By implementing versioning, compatibility, migration, validation, change management, testing, rollback, and recovery strategies, it's possible to manage schema evolution and data versioning effectively and ensure the system's continued functionality and stability.

6.14   How do you approach designing a distributed system with support for advanced data provenance and lineage tracking?

Designing a distributed system with support for advanced data provenance and lineage tracking requires careful consideration of data management, processing, and storage. Data provenance refers to the history of data, including its origin, transformations, and lineage, while data lineage is the data's path through the system, including its inputs, outputs, and transformations.

Here are some key considerations when designing a distributed system with advanced data provenance and lineage tracking:

Capturing data provenance: Data provenance can be captured using different techniques such as metadata, logging, tracing, and tagging. Each approach has its advantages and disadvantages, and the choice of technique depends on the specific requirements and constraints of the system. For example, metadata can be used to capture information about the data, such as its format, size, and source, while logging can capture the activities that created or modified the data.

Integrating data provenance with the processing pipeline: The data provenance and lineage information should be integrated with the processing pipeline to enable traceability and auditing of the data. This integration can be achieved using different mechanisms such as event-driven architectures, message queues, or API calls.

Storing data provenance: The data provenance and lineage information should be stored in a way that is easily accessible and queryable. This storage can be achieved using different techniques such as graph databases, relational databases, or distributed file systems. The choice of storage depends on the size and complexity of the data and the performance requirements of the system.

Managing data lineage: Data lineage should be managed using techniques such as versioning, snapshots, and rollback. These techniques enable the system to maintain different versions of the data and revert to a previous version if necessary.

Ensuring data privacy and security: Advanced data provenance and lineage tracking can raise privacy and security concerns, particularly if sensitive data is involved. The system should be designed to ensure the confidentiality, integrity, and availability of the data, and access to the data should be restricted to authorized users.

For example, a healthcare system that processes sensitive patient data may require advanced data provenance and lineage tracking to ensure compliance with regulatory requirements and enable auditing of the data. The system can capture data provenance using metadata and logging, integrate it with the processing pipeline using event-driven architectures, store it using a distributed file system, manage data lineage using snapshots and rollback, and ensure data privacy and security using encryption and access control mechanisms.

6.15 Can you discuss the challenges and best practices for implementing complex data synchronization techniques, such as operational transformation or conflict-free replicated data types (CRDTs)?

Distributed systems often require complex data synchronization techniques to ensure consistency and availability of data across nodes. Two commonly used techniques for this purpose are Operational Transformation (OT) and Conflict-Free Replicated Data Types (CRDTs).

Operational Transformation is a technique used to manage the concurrent editing of shared objects in a distributed system. In OT, each client maintains a local copy of the shared object, and all updates are performed locally on this copy. When an update is made, it is transformed based on its context to ensure that it is applied correctly and consistently with other concurrent updates. The transformed updates are then sent to the other nodes in the system for further processing.

CRDTs, on the other hand, are a family of data structures that are designed to be replicated across multiple nodes in a distributed system. These structures ensure that updates made at one node are automatically propagated to all other nodes, while maintaining strong consistency guarantees. CRDTs typically use a merge operation to combine updates made at different nodes in the system, ensuring that the final state of the object is consistent across all nodes.

While both techniques are useful in their own way, choosing the right synchronization technique depends on the specific requirements of the system. For instance, if the system requires strong consistency guarantees, CRDTs might be a better option as they ensure that all nodes have the same data. On the other hand, if the system requires real-time collaboration, OT might be a better option as it allows multiple users to edit the same document concurrently.

Some best practices for implementing complex data synchronization techniques in distributed systems include:

Understanding the requirements: The first step in implementing data synchronization techniques is to understand the requirements of the system. This includes understanding the data that needs to be synchronized, the performance requirements of the system, and the consistency guarantees needed.

Choosing the right technique: Once the requirements of the system are understood, the appropriate synchronization technique should be chosen. As mentioned earlier, the choice depends on the specific needs of the system.

Partitioning data: If the data to be synchronized is too large to fit into memory, it can be partitioned into smaller chunks that can be processed independently. This allows for better parallelism and reduces the risk of data loss in case of a failure.

Handling conflicts: In case of conflicts between concurrent updates, the system should have a well-defined strategy for conflict resolution. This can include using timestamps to determine the order of updates, or using consensus algorithms to ensure that conflicting updates are resolved in a consistent manner.

Testing and monitoring: Finally, the system should be thoroughly tested and monitored to ensure that it is working as expected. This includes testing for performance, scalability, and fault-tolerance, as well as monitoring the system for errors and performance issues.

6.16 What are some advanced techniques for optimizing network communication and data transfer in large-scale, distributed systems?

In large-scale distributed systems, network communication and data transfer play a critical role in ensuring high performance, availability, and reliability. Here are some advanced techniques for optimizing network communication and data transfer:

Protocol selection: Choosing the right protocol for a particular task

is essential to optimize network communication. Different protocols have different strengths and weaknesses, and selecting the right
one can make a big difference in system performance. For example,
protocols like TCP are reliable but can have high overhead due to
their built-in error-checking mechanisms, while UDP can offer higher
throughput but may sacrifice reliability.

Compression: Compressing data before transmission can reduce the
amount of data that needs to be sent, resulting in faster transmission
times and reduced network congestion. This technique is especially
useful for large data sets, such as media files or data backups.

Caching: Caching frequently accessed data can help reduce the number of network requests and improve system performance. For example, a content delivery network (CDN) caches static content like
images, videos, and documents closer to end-users, reducing the distance data needs to travel and improving response times.

Load balancing: Distributing traffic across multiple servers using load
balancing techniques can help optimize network communication by
ensuring that no single server is overloaded with requests. This technique can also improve fault tolerance by automatically redirecting
traffic to healthy servers in case of failure.

Peer-to-peer communication: In some cases, peer-to-peer (P2P) communication can be more efficient than traditional client-server models.
P2P systems distribute the processing load across multiple nodes in
the network, reducing the burden on any one machine and improving overall system performance. Examples of P2P systems include
BitTorrent and blockchain networks.

Multi-path communication: By leveraging multiple network paths
simultaneously, multi-path communication can help optimize data
transfer and reduce latency. This technique can be useful in situations
where network connectivity is unreliable or bandwidth is limited.

Data replication: Replicating data across multiple nodes can help
optimize network communication by reducing the distance data needs
to travel and improving availability. This technique is commonly used
in distributed databases and content delivery networks.

Overall, optimizing network communication and data transfer is critical to the performance and reliability of large-scale distributed sys-

tems. By carefully selecting protocols, compressing data, caching frequently accessed content, load balancing, leveraging P2P communication, using multi-path communication, and replicating data, system architects can ensure that their systems can handle large volumes of data efficiently and reliably.

6.17 How do you design a system with support for advanced resource management and allocation, such as workload prioritization or quality of service (QoS) guarantees?

Designing a system with support for advanced resource management and allocation is critical to ensure efficient use of resources and to meet the requirements of different applications and users. Some strategies to achieve this include:

Workload prioritization: This involves assigning different priorities to different workloads or applications based on their criticality and resource requirements. High-priority applications are given access to more resources, while lower-priority applications are allocated fewer resources. This ensures that critical workloads are always prioritized, and less important workloads don't impact system performance.

Resource isolation: This involves isolating resources between different workloads or applications to prevent interference and ensure consistent performance. Resource isolation can be achieved using virtualization technologies, containers, or operating system-level isolation.

Dynamic resource allocation: This involves dynamically allocating resources to different workloads or applications based on their changing requirements. For example, if an application suddenly experiences a spike in traffic, the system can automatically allocate more resources to handle the increased load.

Quality of service (QoS) guarantees: This involves providing guarantees on the level of service provided to different applications or users. QoS guarantees can be based on various metrics, such as latency, throughput, or availability. This ensures that critical applications receive the required level of service, even under high load conditions.

Resource pooling: This involves pooling together resources from multiple sources, such as different servers or data centers, to provide a unified view of resources. Resource pooling enables efficient resource utilization and can help prevent resource wastage.

To design a system with advanced resource management and allocation, it is essential to understand the requirements of different applications and users and to select the appropriate technologies and strategies that best meet those requirements. It is also important to regularly monitor the system's resource usage and adjust resource allocation as needed to ensure optimal performance.

6.18   Can you discuss the challenges and best practices for implementing advanced monitoring and observability features, such as distributed tracing or anomaly detection?

Distributed systems are complex and dynamic, with multiple nodes, services, and components interacting with each other in various ways. Therefore, it's essential to have effective monitoring and observability mechanisms in place to ensure system health, performance, and availability. In this context, advanced monitoring and observability features, such as distributed tracing and anomaly detection, can be particularly useful for identifying and diagnosing issues in distributed systems.

Distributed tracing is a technique for tracking the flow of requests across multiple services and components in a distributed system. It provides a way to trace the lifecycle of a request from its origin to its destination, including all the intermediary services and components that the request goes through. Distributed tracing typically involves adding unique identifiers (e.g., correlation IDs) to requests as they enter the system and propagating these identifiers across all subsequent requests and responses. By analyzing the collected traces, it's possible to identify the bottlenecks, errors, and performance issues in the system and optimize its behavior accordingly. Popular distributed tracing systems include OpenTracing, Jaeger, and Zipkin.

Anomaly detection is another advanced monitoring and observability technique that can help detect unusual patterns or events in distributed systems. Anomalies can indicate performance issues, security breaches, or other unexpected behaviors that need attention. Anomaly detection typically involves analyzing various metrics and events across the system and identifying deviations from expected patterns or baselines. Machine learning and statistical techniques can be used to automate the detection and alerting of anomalies. For example, Prometheus is an open-source monitoring system that includes support for anomaly detection based on time-series data.

Some best practices for implementing advanced monitoring and observability features in distributed systems include:

Define meaningful metrics and alerts: It's important to choose metrics that are relevant to the system's performance and behavior and define alerts that can trigger appropriate responses based on the severity and impact of the issues detected.

Use distributed tracing to capture end-to-end request flows: Distributed tracing can help identify bottlenecks, latency issues, and error paths in a distributed system. It's important to instrument all critical components and services to capture accurate and complete traces.

Leverage machine learning and statistical techniques for anomaly detection: Machine learning and statistical techniques can help automate the detection of anomalies and reduce the time and effort required for manual analysis. However, it's important to validate and fine-tune the models to avoid false positives and negatives.

Implement a centralized logging and metrics aggregation system: A centralized logging and metrics aggregation system can simplify the collection, storage, and analysis of monitoring data across the system. It's important to choose a system that can handle the scale and complexity of the data and provide easy access and visualization capabilities.

Integrate monitoring and observability with the development and deployment pipeline: Monitoring and observability should be an integral part of the development and deployment pipeline to ensure that the system is continuously tested and monitored in various environments and scenarios. Tools such as GitLab and Jenkins can be used to automate monitoring and observability tasks as part of the CI/CD pipeline.

In summary, advanced monitoring and observability features, such as distributed tracing and anomaly detection, can provide valuable insights into the performance, behavior, and health of distributed systems. However, implementing these features requires careful planning, instrumentation, and validation to ensure their effectiveness and reliability.

6.19 What are some advanced strategies for managing system complexity and technical debt in large-scale, distributed systems?

Large-scale distributed systems can become complex and difficult to manage over time, especially as new features are added, and changes are made to the architecture. Technical debt, the accumulation of suboptimal design decisions and shortcuts, can also compound this complexity, making it harder to maintain and evolve the system. Therefore, it's important to adopt advanced strategies for managing system complexity and technical debt. Some of these strategies include:

Adopting good software design principles: Well-designed software should be modular, loosely coupled, and highly cohesive. By following these principles, developers can build systems that are easier to understand, test, and maintain. For example, a modular system can be broken down into smaller, more manageable parts, while a loosely coupled system can minimize the impact of changes made to one part of the system on other parts of the system.

Emphasizing good software testing practices: Testing is essential for ensuring that a system is functioning as expected and that changes to the system do not introduce new bugs. Adopting good testing practices such as automated testing, continuous integration, and continuous delivery can help minimize technical debt and prevent complexity from getting out of control.

Applying agile software development methodologies: Agile methodologies emphasize the iterative and incremental development of software, which can help prevent complexity and technical debt from accumulating over time. By breaking down development into smaller, more manageable chunks, developers can focus on delivering functionality quickly while minimizing the risk of introducing new problems.

Using containerization and microservices: Containerization and microservices can help simplify the deployment and management of large-scale distributed systems. By breaking down a system into smaller, more isolated components, it becomes easier to manage and maintain each component separately. Containerization, in particular, can help streamline deployment by ensuring that each component has its own isolated runtime environment.

Adopting cloud-native technologies: Cloud-native technologies, such as Kubernetes and cloud-native databases, can help simplify the deployment and management of large-scale distributed systems in cloud environments. These technologies provide advanced features such as auto-scaling, automatic failover, and self-healing, which can help prevent complexity and technical debt from accumulating over time.

Embracing observability and monitoring: Observability and monitoring are critical for managing large-scale distributed systems. By adopting advanced monitoring and observability techniques such as distributed tracing, anomaly detection, and log analysis, developers can gain a deeper understanding of how the system is performing, and quickly identify and resolve issues before they become major problems.

In conclusion, managing system complexity and technical debt is critical for the success of large-scale distributed systems. By adopting good software design principles, testing practices, agile methodologies, containerization, cloud-native technologies, and observability and monitoring techniques, developers can build and maintain systems that are reliable, scalable, and easy to manage over time.

6.20   Can you discuss the challenges and best practices for implementing advanced distributed consensus algorithms and protocols, such as Byzantine fault tolerance or blockchain-based consensus?

Distributed consensus algorithms are used in distributed systems to reach a consensus on a particular decision or value, even when some of the nodes in the system are faulty or fail. These algorithms play a critical role in ensuring the integrity and consistency of the system, and they are used in a variety of applications, including distributed databases, blockchain networks, and distributed file systems.

One of the most well-known consensus algorithms is the Paxos algorithm, which is used to achieve consensus in a distributed system with multiple nodes. In this algorithm, each node proposes a value and then participates in a series of rounds of voting to determine which value should be accepted. In each round, nodes communicate with each other and try to reach a quorum, which is a threshold of nodes that must agree on a value for it to be accepted.

Another consensus algorithm is the Raft algorithm, which is designed to be more understandable and easier to implement than Paxos. The Raft algorithm also uses a leader-based approach, where a leader node is responsible for coordinating the consensus process. In Raft, nodes elect a leader, and then the leader proposes a value that the other nodes must agree on.

Byzantine fault tolerance is a more advanced consensus protocol that is used in systems where nodes may be malicious or intentionally fail to follow the protocol. In these systems, it is critical to have a consensus algorithm that can detect and correct for Byzantine failures. Byzantine fault tolerance algorithms use various techniques, such as digital signatures and quorums, to ensure that only correct nodes are included in the consensus process.

Blockchain-based consensus algorithms are used in blockchain networks, where nodes must agree on the ordering and content of transactions in the network. In these systems, consensus is achieved through a process called mining, where nodes compete to solve a cryptographic puzzle, and the first node to solve the puzzle is rewarded with new cryptocurrency tokens. This process ensures that only one version of the blockchain exists and that all nodes agree on its content.

Implementing advanced distributed consensus algorithms and protocols comes with many challenges. One of the most significant challenges is ensuring that the protocol can handle failures and errors, such as network delays, node failures, or malicious attacks. Another challenge is achieving scalability and performance, as consensus algorithms can become increasingly complex and resource-intensive as the number of nodes in the system grows.

To address these challenges, best practices for implementing advanced distributed consensus algorithms and protocols include careful design and testing, fault tolerance and recovery mechanisms, and careful consideration of network and system architecture. Additionally, implementing these algorithms often requires a deep understanding of distributed systems and cryptography, as well as experience with low-level systems programming and networking.

Made in the USA
Monee, IL
08 January 2025